Expanding the Rainbow:
My Road to Adopting a Baby with Down Syndrome

Expanding the Rainbow:
My Road to Adopting a Baby with Down Syndrome

Sarah-Jane Cavilry

Sarah-Jane Cavilry
2015

First Printing: 2015
ISBN 978-1-312-81865-1
Sarah-Jane Cavilry
expandingtherainbow@gmail.com

To My Little Mouse

Thank you to all of the real-life characters who joined us on the adventure called life to create this true story. Names and other identifying information in this book have been changed to protect the confidentiality of some participants.

I would like to give the sincerest thanks to the people in my life who have always loved, accepted, and supported my quirky little family: A.M. and S. S., Melodrama Liz, the Freeman cousins, Toreador 'terps, past coworkers (Denise, Naomi, Kathy, Janet C-P, Amber, Dena, Stephanie H, Janet M, Brooke, Billie, Gabe, Chris), Anna, Tess, Linda M., everyone at KCC, M.A.R.C., Ronnie, my stepfather, my stepmother, and my wonderful dad. Thanks, Bro, for all the book help. Thank you, Mom, for organizing my life. To my awesome husband, I love you.

In loving memory of my mother-in-law.

Introduction

Life is like being lost in the woods, walking down a long, unfamiliar path. Along the way, there are forks of two, three, maybe even 10 diverging paths, and we constantly have to decide which one is the best to take in order to get to where we need to go. One path might lead immediately to something long wished for; another path might lead to sorrow or regret. But each path chosen will lead to another path, and another, and another, and decisions must be made at the forks.

My figurative hike through the woods hasn't been terribly bumpy or hilly. There was never any path that led me through anything as difficult as an ascent up Mount Everest; maybe one or two like a climb down the Grand Canyon and back up the other side, leaving me tired and achy, even spiritually changed, but certainly happy that I was back out and on the other side of that particular excursion. But now that I'm at the end of my most recent journey, I can say, without a doubt, that I am happy with every decision I've made at my life's forks because, even if things seemed bad at the time, the paths led me to where I am now, and I am overjoyed with the outcome.

Chapter 1:

The Dance

At four years old, a suitable age for a variety of parentally-induced extracurricular activities, my mother enrolled me in a Spanish-dancing class. As a flaming ginger in a dance class dedicated to a Hispanic musical genre, I had the potential to stand out like the white sheep in a pasture of ebony locks. But as classes took place in Pine Valley, one of the whitest places in California in the early '70s, I was one of two redheads and six blondes prancing energetically to the Latin beats. Weekly rehearsals with a tall, beautiful Latina teacher culminated in bi-yearly costumed ensemble stage performances. I loved these events—puffy skirts, spray-painted shoes, flower-bedecked hair, bright red lipstick, and the clickety-clacking flair of castanets as I twirled and stamped. I relished prancing and posing in front of the smiling crowds.

The performances were in different locations around the county, allowing for a variety of audience types—parents, other adults, school children, seniors. My mother prepared me for one of these seasonal engagements by imparting me with a little information concerning this particular audience:

"The show you're dancing in today will be at a school for special kids."

Rather than using any of the more callous labels that were still fairly acceptable in the current era, my mother was far ahead of her time. Phrasing aside, I had never heard an entire school of children described as "special." I rolled the word around in my head for a few moments before asking, "What's special mean?"

"Well," Mom replied with cheerful matter-of-factness, "they're kids who learn things more slowly than normal children. They're a little different from us. It's going to be a lot of fun dancing for them.

They'll probably love seeing all the colorful costumes." Mom tossed the novel concept to me with such a casual optimism, I was induced to believe that these spectators would have an innate enjoyment of watching me dance and seeing my flowing costume whirl around me. The idea of an audience that would love me even more than the norm made my egotistical little performer-self very glad.

Backstage, while my mom fastened a grand orange flower to the top of my curled and hair-sprayed ponytail, I pointed at some drawings fixed to the dressing room wall. "Look," I observed, "someone drew pictures of people from the Wizard of Oz." Dorothy, the Scarecrow, the Cowardly Lion, the Tin Man, and even the Wicked Witch were all represented in colorful, detailed portraiture. I distinctly remember that the characters' countenances were very serious, and very lifelike.

"They look real."

"Yes, don't they?" Mom noted with an admiring smile. "Sometimes special people are very artistic."

I didn't realize that someone special and slow had made those drawings. This phenomenon impressed me, that someone who was special had made something so vivid and accomplished. These students were, allegedly, different from me, but, along with skills they lacked, they had evident abilities, even some exceptional talents.

When the introductory notes of my dance group's musical piece sounded over the auditorium speakers, I entered the stage, posed in readiness, and began dancing as rehearsed, stepping and turning in unison with the rest of the flaxen niños and niñas of my class. As was my personal custom, I watched the audience's reaction to our frolicking adorableness. But on this evening, for the first time, I saw the special people. They were probably situated throughout the audience, but as my memory was recorded through the eye of a five or six year old, I only recollect the patrons seated in the front row—young adults, not little kids as I had been expecting. Right off, I noticed these big kids really were different from me, as Mom had forewarned. One young man clapped and laughed loudly, regarding more of the floor in front of him than my movements behind the spotlight. Near him, a woman rocked in her wheelchair, her head slowly oscillating back and forth while she punctuated the air with sporadic whooping noises. Another young man was swaying, Weeblestyle, either to our Latin rhythms or a beat of his own, a huge grin on his youthful face.

I wasn't sure why they were doing what they were doing, but they didn't seem unhappy. To my inexperienced eyes, they appeared to be enjoying themselves—having a pretty awesome time, in fact. I came to the conclusion that their percussive sounds and quirky movements were their way of enjoying the show. Rather than sitting quietly, hands folded in laps, their uniqueness freed them to let loose and enjoy the show without reserve. And just maybe one of them had drawn those Oz pictures.

I contemplated those people for the rest of the day. Honestly, I've never forgotten them. In only a few off-hand sentences of introduction, my mother had unwittingly initiated my life-long interest in people with disabilities—individuals who were not the everyday walking-and-talking-just-like-me types, but who had various talents and pleasures and creative ways of presenting themselves. A life-long fascination was the result.

Throughout my childhood, Mom continued to point out people with various mental and anatomical anomalies—the woman in a wheelchair with long gold fingernails; a little girl who had braces on her legs and was so tiny and adorable. But my favorite people were always the ones with developmental disabilities: the boy who was a little slow and had a beloved pet dog that he walked daily; the young adult with Down syndrome who so lovingly held her elderly mom's hand. Retaining the memory of the Oz drawings, I continued to be captivated by what special people could do and how they did it. In third grade, when I filled out a class worksheet that asked, "What do you want to be when you grow up?" I wrote, "I want to work with retarded kids." When I rediscovered that sheet as an adult, I was completely unsurprised that I had written such a comment.

My mom was a consistent, fun, creative influence, who nurtured my curiosity in the many topics I found fascinating as a child. Whenever I blurted out the common childhood phrase, "I'm bored," she would come up with a plethora of delightful, age-appropriate, clever ideas for diverse pretend play. Chopsticks at a Japanese restaurant would become a man with wide-stanced, wobbly legs. An old tape recorder would be a conduit through which I could chronicle lengthy, elaborate stories. When luck was with me, Mom would use my persistent demands for entertainment as an excuse for a tea party with her best china set. We would pour hot chocolate with an elegant alabaster teapot and serve the sugary, lukewarm concoction in tiny white teacups. I always appreciated my mom's ability to spontaneously invent imaginative alternatives to boredom.

Mom not only taught me about creative play, but also about creative thought, especially how fantasy might translate into reality. Talking about the stars in the night sky might evolve into a discourse about what it must be like to be an astronaut exploring the universe first-hand. Watching a deaf person use signs would prompt Mom to suggest it might be fun to learn that language and converse manually. Before the days of fertility treatments and the commonality of multiples, seeing a mother on the street holding the hands of two little identical siblings would cause my mom to exclaim, "Oh look, twins! I always thought it would be fun to have twins. Who knows—maybe you'll have twins one day."

Mom divulged an account of a little girl who was attending our local elementary school, was seven years old, and needed to be adopted. She said that the girl would probably never be successfully adopted because, being seven, she was too old. Prospective parents, in search of the full parenting experience, tended to adopt infant children. I expressed how satisfying it would be to adopt a child like that girl, a child who was having a hard time finding a home, and mom agreed that, although not possible for us at the moment, perhaps I could help a motherless child when I grew up.

I loved these hypothetical musings. David Bowie's "Major Tom" took the joy out of space flight fantasies, but I still liked to think about all the other future adulthood possibilities. I fantasized often about the prospect of giving birth to twins or adopting a grateful, needing child.

In fact, I did grow up to have twins. Despite the heartbreaking reality that they were stillborn, I always felt as if they were meant to be, as their existence had brought to fruition one of my regular childhood contemplations. Their lives were cut short, but they were concrete proof that dreams do come true.

Unbeknownst to her, Mom's ability to think outside the box also sparked my personal philosophical outlook that, with a little creative processing, most anything is possible.

Chapter 2:
Christopher

When I was 15, my brother had a girlfriend around my age, Debbie, who worked at a neighborhood home for disabled children in Westview. When she told me the boss was seeking an additional employee, I thought that applying for the position sounded like a really fun idea. I had been thinking about getting a job so I could have some extra spending money to keep me current and fashionable with all the totally rad styles of the '80s. An added incentive to work at the home was that Debbie and I got along well and always had a good laugh in each other's company. Most of all, I remembered the happy, laughing, clapping special people in the front row of the audience at the Spanish-dance recital. This job sounded like an intriguing prospect.

Debbie invited me to visit her one afternoon while she was on the clock so that I could meet the kids, introduce myself to her boss, and see if I wanted to apply for the job. When Debbie opened the door to welcome me into the front entrance, the smell that wafted out the door reminded me of when we used to visit my senile 98-year-old grandmother at the old-folks' home, that unmistakable aroma of cleanser, urine, and closed windows. I blinked and smiled while Debbie invited me in and led me through the foyer, past the kitchen, and directly to the back bedroom where all six child residents were situated for the morning. I tried not to react outwardly, but seeing the kids for the first time was quite shocking.

The children were placed in various locations around the perimeter of the tan-carpeted bedroom-turned-recroom, perched on low-sitting padded chairs or placed supine on foam wedges. Each of them stayed in the same spot where they had been deposited, making random, jerky motions, rolling their heads from side to side, slowly bending and unbending their arms and legs in movements which appeared involuntary and purposeless. As a whole, the group looked like a Petri dish full of wriggling, mutant specimens, like two-tailed sperm that wiggle and rotate in slow circles.

Across the room, placed in the corner, a 9-year-old boy was lying in a cheap blue outdoor-type one-summer's-use plastic swimming pool filled with dozens of balls in assorted, bright, primary colors. His hands were tightly clenched and bent so far back that his wrists had completely popped out of joint, and his lips were parted to allow the liberation of a constant stream of drool from the corner of his mouth. He made no movements at all except for slowly rotating his head from side to side.

Adjacent to the swimming pool, another boy was lying on a large off-white foam wedge under an infant's mobile that he didn't seem to notice. His head was turned hard to the right, and his entire body was rigid—his hands were at his sides, fists clenched, legs straight, feet flexed, and all said parts were as stiff as wooden planks. He never, ever stopped crying a loud, whining, emotionless moan with a pained, desperate look in his eyes. Occasionally, Debbie or another worker would go over to the boy and start violently shaking his leg back and forth. The stiffness of his muscles made his whole body follow along for the jerky ride. The callous action seemed shocking at first, but the worker explained, "It's the only thing that makes him stop crying." And it really did. The moment the worker stopped yanking his limb to tend to another resident, the sad child started crying again.

To the left of the wooden boy, there was a little girl who had the sunken, misty eyes of someone who was obviously blind. She was about the size of a three-month-old, but was actually a full five years of age. Rather than enrolling in kindergarten and mastering her ABCs, she spent her time strapped in an infant's car seat, playfully kicking her feet, clasping her hands together, giggling to herself, and occasionally putting one set of fingertips down her throat to stimulate her own gag reflex. Debbie told me they were glad the girl had stopped compulsively making herself actually throw up.

A properly-sized nine-year-old was lying prone in the middle of the floor. She lay quietly for several minutes, vomited, and continued to rest, not budging to get away from the resulting mess beneath her cheek. Debbie cleaned her up and put a blue plastic pad under her head in preparation for any upcoming messes.

I glanced a few more times around the room, not exactly sure where to rest my gaze, pretending to look happily at the adorable beings writhing around my feet. When I looked over my shoulder, there was Debbie holding yet another child.

I was taken aback. He looked, honestly, frightening. His immobile arms lay parallel to his sides, rigidly resisting gravity's downward pull. His head, although appropriate in size for his age of one year, was, when compared to his body, enormous—about as large as his torso, and as wide as his shoulders.

"Here's Christopher! Isn't he *cute*?" She presented the boy to me like a proud adoptive mother.

Debbie invited me to sit on the small leather couch in the adjoining office so that I might have a turn holding the unfortunate child. Although I was wary, afraid that I might break some part of his disabled form, Debbie placed Christopher in my arms. I looked into his bright blue eyes and he stared back at me.

We gazed at each other. Christopher and me.

"Touch his forehead," Debbie ordered with enthusiasm. "Just put your fingers on his forehead."

Debbie authoritatively standing over me, I peered up questioningly before lightly caressing Christopher just above the eyebrows. Slowly, he began rocking his head from side to side, enjoying the soft tickling sensation of my fingertips on his delicate skin. He even closed his eyes and let out a barely audible squeak of pleasure, like a tiny baby monkey being lovingly groomed.

I looked up at Debbie and, with eyes wide and grin beaming, exclaimed, "Oh…my…*God*!"

"I *know*!" was her almost-shrieked response as she hopped in place, hands clasped together in adolescent ecstasy. It was unanimous; Christopher had been voted by us teens—the most valid vote of all—to be adorable.

Debbie led me into the various rooms of the home to see the rest of the facilities and finish meeting the other children. Looking back at Christopher, now tucked under a blanket in his crib for a nap, I realized my decision had already been made. I applied for and got the job.

The owner and director of the home was a warm and caring woman, Bernadette. I admired her greatly. Not only was she an RN, an admirable profession on its own—you have to look up to anyone who cares about people so much that they go to school to study blood and feces—but she had brought six of the most disabled humans I had ever seen into her home to care for and give the best life possible. I was awed by her goodness.

The only problem was—she had married Walid. Walid hadn't studied anything as far as I knew, and appeared to have only feelings of annoyance toward the juvenile creatures infesting his home. He didn't know the tiniest thing about caring for disabled children, but he wanted to be the boss—in charge; therefore, he constantly told the workers what to do with the children, and his instructions were always questionable. Although the children all only had physical disabilities, Walid told me not to hug any of the children to avoid passing their diseases around. When the muscle control of the young boy from the blue plastic pool—Manny, actually—made feeding him a time-consuming task, Walid told me not to waste time and just push the food into the boy's mouth faster. When the weather was hot, Walid told me to rub the children's backs with ice cubes. When more than one child cried at a time (which was at least once daily), Walid would throw open the door and, with his best angry-and-suspicious glare, look slowly around the room from child to child and worker to worker as if to say, "What the hell is being done wrong?" The one thing he did like about the childcare business was being able to take the wheelchair-accessible van out to the store and park it in the conveniently available and proximal handicapped parking spot. For all the drool and poo and barf I had to deal with at that job, there was nothing grosser than Walid.

Over time, spending four or five hours at the home several days a week, I got to know all of the kids very well. Of the six children living there, none were able to walk. All were in diapers. One little girl could speak a few words, although her comprehension was questionable. Most all the residents had seizure disorders.

I peeked at their files one evening and saw their diagnoses; I was shocked by what I discovered. When the mother was pregnant with Manny, her water broke and the doctor told her to go home and not worry about it; he was finally born a month later, severely brain damaged, the doctor was sued, and Manny became a millionaire who would never know it. The girl who could speak a few words, Kelly, was birthed by a mother who hid the pregnancy and never went to the doctor, leaving the large hematoma in her baby's umbilical cord undetected; Kelly was born blue and soon abandoned by her mother. The wooden boy, Kyle, was vaccinated when he was sick with a high fever. The little blind five-year-old, Samantha, was born premature, so her ignorant parents tried to help her gain strength by feeding her raw eggs and honey. The girl who vomited on the floor and didn't move, Nikki, had been riding her tricycle around the pool unattended when she fell in and went without oxygen for 20 minutes. All the parents of these children decided to have them placed full-time in residential care. All parents either rarely or never visited.

My initial impressions long since pushed aside, I came to realize that all of these children had their own personalities, likes and dislikes, and through the years of working with them, I grew to deeply love every last one. I'd take Nikki shopping for new clothes every year on her birthday. I'd tickle Samantha and make her infectiously giggle. I'd ask Kelly to identify the correct colored block, and I'd cheer wildly, to her delight, when she got it right. I'd whisper sweetly into Manny's ear and see him become quiet with recognition. The disabilities of these people were not their faults. In fact, some of their disabilities were the direct fault of others. These blameless children all deserved to have the best lives possible from then on. And they deserved lots of hugs.

I didn't know at the time, but some of those children were also very ill, the prognoses being that they would probably not live to adulthood. When Debbie called me at home to say that Christopher had died, we cried together, knowing we would never again feel the joy of holding his tiny body in our arms. It was exceptional that Christopher had lived to the age of one, his growing organs quickly running out of space within his tiny frame. One year may have been the extent of his destiny, but it was also our delight. Although our time together was short, my connection with Christopher remains a cherished memory.

After being employed there for a couple years, Nikki grew too large to be cared for at Bernadette's home any longer. I went to work, ready to give her a secret morning hug, to find her and all her belongings gone. She was moved to a facility in Pasadena and nobody thought I needed to be forewarned. I certainly would have appreciated the opportunity to say goodbye. Instead, the last time I had seen her ended up being the last time I would ever see her. A new child immediately took her place at our facility.

The new tenant, three-year-old Les, was born to adoring, devoted parents. Doctors quickly discovered that the beloved son had multiple disabilities, including a profound seizure disorder and severe mental retardation. After trying unsuccessfully to care for him at home, the heartbroken couple decided the most caring way to support the welfare of their boy would be to have him reside permanently in Bernadette's facility.

Although Les came to us after his third birthday, he looked much younger than his chronological age. His small, delicate frame could be easily cradled in one arm. Despite the fact that his body was properly proportioned, his spindly limbs gave him a bony vulnerability. Like most of the other residents, he didn't talk; like all of the residents, he didn't walk. Furthermore, Les was blind. His sightless eyes, though, had all the power of expression necessary to communicate his emotions. Little Les' emotions were surprisingly varied: sad, happy, uncomfortable, content, heartbroken, and loved. But the negative emotions were the ones that affected him most overwhelmingly. Emotional or physical stress, from the aggravation of hot weather to the mental disturbance of being separated from his parents, could trigger an excruciating series of seizures.

Though profoundly developmentally disabled, he loved his parents, especially his dear mother. He realized when she was there, as well as when she was gone. At the conclusion of a visit, the resulting absence of his mother would usually bring Les the most acute distress imaginable, manifested in a continuous onslaught of torturing seizures. On these lonesome occasions, several times throughout the day, Les would emit a low moan that would increase to a loud cry, reaching its zenith at a sustained, terrified scream. Mirroring the progression of his shrieks, his prone body would begin to bend, his torso arching back until his head pointed toward his heels, his body becoming a solid, rounded arc, like the runner of a rocking chair. The convulsion would last 15 to 30 seconds, ending in a relaxation of his muscles and an audible exhalation of air. Les would lie on the floor, momentarily tranquil, until his next impending seizure.

Bad days like these resulted in repeated seizures with short one- or two-minute respites in between. On good days, the seizures would come only a few times every hour. As a result, both types of days probably ended up feeling pretty rotten for our unlucky little guy.

Despite this monstrous description—spindly, bony, screaming, convulsing—I look back on Les and remember softness. Almost literally, Les was fluffy. He had thick, dark black hair that I loved to run my fingers through. His upper back and sideburns—due to the medications he took—had a soft, light, downy black fuzz that made him feel like a baby animal or cuddly stuffed toy. His eyebrows were thick and connected in the middle with a dollop of dark, feathery fluff. He had eyelashes any woman would die for—thick, long, gently curled, and jet-black.

I loved his eyes the most. When Les was happy, he would tilt his chin up, look skyward with those soulful brown eyes, and softly coo. I was told once by a coworker that Les' mother, in an attempt to make the task of eating easier for his weak body, would hold him on her lap, tilt his chin up, and let the food slowly run down his throat. Someone in the medical profession might believe this method of feeding a severely disabled baby to be less than ideal. However, Les' mother was doing what she thought was best, and she was doing it with love. Les must have been able to sense the love in her hands; for Les, the chin-raised position was an expression of love between mother and son.

On an unbearably hot night, I was putting the children to bed but could not console Les enough to stop his seizing and bring sleep. When all the other residents were in their cribs, diapered, pajamaed, and ready for dreamland, I went to Les' bedside and lifted him from the mattress. Bringing him to a chair in the nursery, I sat him on my lap and held him, silently. I didn't sing or talk—I just held him and rocked. Then—I'll never forget the image of him on my knee—he tilted his chin upward, opened his eyes wide, and cooed for me. He was happy, and I had comforted him. That moment was, at 18 years old, my first experience of motherly affection—maternal instinct—a tender connection with a child. I fell in love with Les at that second.

In high school, I was in the advanced-placement, invitation-only drawing class. I spent a lot of time perfecting graphite portraits of my favorite people, mostly for school assignments, occasionally for myself or friends. I had previously taken a Polaroid photograph of Les' mom holding the boy, the I-love-Mama, eyes-uplifted expression on his face. After a failing trial run, I finally drew and perfected a portrait of Les that I was happy with, put it in a manila envelope, and left it for his mom to pick up on her next visit to the home. The following week, my coworker told me that when Les' mom opened the envelope and saw the drawing, she cried. I hoped the time I had taken on the artwork helped her understand that our love for Les was mutual.

Being a full-time high school student, I only worked 20 hours per week at the home, often with three or four days off in a row. During one such period with no work, I arrived home after some time shopping at the local mall with my high school girlfriends. Toting a store bag from Contempo Casuals and a new, oversized white belt, I walked into my dad's home office to gleefully announce, "I'm back!"

Off-handedly, he replied, "Oh, someone from your work called to say Les died."

Before bursting into inconsolable sobs, I screamed, "*Why?*"

My response was reflexive and immediate. I knew my dad wouldn't have the answer, but I asked it just the same.

With a look of surprise, Dad responded, "I don't know," instantly regretting his own nonchalance. My severe reaction succinctly informed Dad, never speaking with me of Les before, what that child's name meant to me. I soon found out, nobody had really known the depth of my love for that boy.

The next time I went to work, I spent the main portion of my shift looking at the company photo album, seeking any image of Les, beholding each one for five, ten, fifteen minutes, wishing for another moment with him in my arms, peering up at me with those soulful eyes just one last time.

When I wrote down the incidents of the day in the program aides' journal, I read the entries from previous shifts and found that Les had actually died and had his funeral several days before I was informed of his passing. I wasn't considered an important enough figure in Les' life to be notified until he was already removed from the home and made resident of a cemetery. The sting of loss increased exponentially.

After giving Les' mom the portrait, I had not had an occasion to see her again—and then her son died. Although nobody in my midst at the time knew what that boy meant to me, I hope, at the very least, his mother knew.

I heard, many months later, that Les' parents had a new little girl. The baby had some minor medical problems, but was otherwise healthy, already learning to toddle around the kitchen. I was relieved for the mourning and healing parents, and I mentally bestowed wishes of a life filled with happiness to Les' mommy, daddy, and baby sister.

Chapter 3:

The Boys

Bernadette also owned an additional site nearby in Fieldpark where I would occasionally substitute for a worker who was ill or on vacation. This second facility housed older children and young adult residents with varying degrees of mental retardation. It was here that I first personally encountered people with autism and Down syndrome.

Among the autistic residents of the home, there were two young boys, Jeffrey and Todd, whom I remember with particular fondness. Jeffrey was the youngest tenant, a nine-year-old boy with a blonde bowl-haircut and an adorable gap between his buckteeth. His daily goal, from the time he awoke to the time he went to bed, was to locate and procure string. He was fixated on string or anything resembling string: a piece of yarn, a broken rubber band, a thread from his clothes. But his greatest joy was the jump rope that was kept on the top shelf of the playroom. The workers were instructed to keep the rope away from Jeffrey, as well as other string-like objects he found, because the facility supervisor Glenda—wife of Walid's brother, Hari—believed that Jeffrey should be refused access to this obsession.

Although regularly diverted from the jump rope, Jeffrey would, several times a day, guide me over to the toy area. He would grasp my arm and lead me across the room until I was standing beneath the shelf. Then he'd pushed my elbow upward until my arm extended toward the baskets of toys near the top of the wall. I would respond to his request by grabbing the nearest toy and offering it to him. Expressionless, he would hold it momentarily before dropping it on the floor. As he'd repeatedly guided my arm upward, over and over again, I would hand him toy after toy, replicating the procedure until my hand finally appeared before his eyes with his beloved rope.

Identifying and taking the prize, Jeffrey would show no emotional response, simply pivoting and planting himself in an overstuffed chair with his conquest in his lap, making circles, loops, and squiggles. Every time we performed this ritual, I felt like Jeffrey and I were sharing a moment of connection, which struck me as touching and warmly engaging. It was always the same routine. I'd take everything off the shelf except what I knew he wanted. The single time that I did give him the rope, I was instructed to keep this favored toy out of his reach. I saw no harm in letting him play with the jump rope or any other rope or string, as it only brought him serenity while he sat in quiet contentment playing with the treasure. I hated that facility policy demanded this refusal. I have since heard that, as autism becomes better understood, some professionals no longer see deprivation as an unquestionable requirement for dealing with certain fixations. As an adult, had I been involved in the field of autism, I would probably have been one of those professionals.

Todd, the second autistic boy at this care home, was a tall, thin, 12-year-old with a pale, hauntingly expressionless countenance. Todd, too, spent his days sitting in a beige overstuffed chair in the living room, but he never interacted with other workers or children, nor did he play with any toys. Every morning, from the moment he was removed from bed, dressed by a worker, led into the recreation room, and situated in the chair, he would raise his hands to his face, about an inch from his eyes, and begin moving his fingers back and forth in slow, repetitive waving motions, like sea grass swaying rhythmically on the ocean floor. Todd would do this silently, peacefully, and constantly for hours at a time. (Luckily, I wasn't instructed to keep his fingers on the top shelf.)

Every two hours, I would take Todd by the arm, stand him up, and guide him to the restroom, where I would prepare him to sit on the toilet. He would follow me robotically, without protest, seemingly ignorant of the fact that he was moving from one room to the next. Once he was seated on the commode, I'd stand at the sink and wait for up to 20 minutes until I heard a tinkling sound. Then, I would raise him to his feet, redress him, and return him to the playroom chair. There, he would recommence waving his fingers in front of his eyes. At mealtimes, I would place Todd in front of a bowl at the head of the dining room table so he could mindlessly shovel food into his mouth with a thick-handled spoon. Then I'd guide him back to his chair for more finger-waving time. These rituals occurred and recurred every day in complete silence; I never talked with Todd or even considered trying.

On a warm summer Saturday, Glenda took all the residents and some staff on an outing to a local pizza parlor. All of the young men and women in our care were excited about the trip to town, except for Todd, who didn't appear to care one way or the other. He allowed himself to be directed into the restaurant, and he ate when he was presented with food. The rest of the time, he didn't seem to even notice that he wasn't at home.

After a slice or two of pepperoni and a dollars-worth of videogames, our troop began heading back to the car. As we walked through the parking lot, someone behind me began singing an unmelodic, droning rendition of an excerpt from a familiar children's song.

"E –I – E – I – O…E – I – E – I – O…"

I whipped my head around to discover that the soloist, being steered through the parking lot by an unimpressed female program aide, was Todd. His head was pointed straight forward, gaze unfocused, but evidently, indicated by the outburst of song, he was happy. I hadn't previously known he was capable of any type of vocalization or emotion, but now I thought an attempt at communicating with him might be worth trying.

The next time I traversed with Todd to the bathroom, instead of impatiently and silently leaning against the sink waiting for him to make a tinkle, I looked at him and sang,

"Old Mac Donald had a farm, E – I – E – I – O."

Todd slowly turned his head, looked me directly in the eye, and presented me with a lopsided grin. The moment of connection was brief, but adorably warm and personal. Through that experience, I learned about Todd's ability to connect with others. I'd soon find out that my new knowledge of Todd's true character and ability to connect was as small as a single blade of waving sea grass at the bottom of the Atlantic.

On Todd's birthday, his father came to visit. As always, Todd had no motivation to leave his favorite chair, so a staff member led the birthday boy to the front door. When Dad appeared in the foyer, Todd paused and looked blankly at the man.

Then, recognition set in. Todd suddenly burst into a running-in-place sort of dance, leaped at his father, and threw his arms around his beloved daddy's neck. Todd spent the next hour back in his playroom chair, but now sitting on his father's lap, not even bothering with finger-waving.

Todd wasn't stupid; he knew where the love was.

Chapter 4:

The Girls

In addition to the autistic residents, three young women with Down syndrome lived at the second care home. They shared the same chromosomal abnormality, but that was where their similarities ended.

Missy, a bespectacled 13-year-old young lady with short, curly, dark-brown hair and fair skin, would tell long, detailed stories about her life experiences. Angeline, a chubby teen with thick, perpetually-dirty glasses, would repeatedly stick out her tongue and chortle. Carolina, age 14, petite with long, straight, blonde hair and a quiet disposition, could say only one word—fish. All three ladies had their charm, their likes and dislikes, and their ability to make me delight in their presence.

Carolina, if she felt a moment of emotional connection with me, would slam and hold her palm against my eyes in an involuntary black-out until I could pry her fingers off my face. Angeline would go into the garage-turned-rumpus-room and repeatedly play, "My Sharona" on an old turntable. Missy loved dancing in a repetitive kick-right, kick-left style, and she sang "The Sound of Silence" in perfect pitch. Interactions with these three were entertaining and fun, and filled me with peace. I relished my times with them and looked forward to every visit. It was during my encounters with Missy, Angeline, and Carolina that I discovered my affection for Down syndrome and the people who carry that extra 21st chromosome.

Individuals with Down syndrome have a reputation for being perpetually cheerful and easy-going, constantly hugging and rarely, if ever, crying. The average layman may be led to believe that these folks walk around with smiles plastered onto their faces, embracing and high-fiving friends and strangers alike, despite the specific situation. But the stereotype that they are eternally happy is erroneous. Folks with Down syndrome have good days and bad days, and they can be blue or downright depressed.

One of my coworkers and her boyfriend brought Carolina on an excursion to a local restaurant. After the trip, I watched as Carolina's chaperones pulled their white pick-up truck back into the driveway of the care home; Carolina sat, red-faced, between the worker and boyfriend, her eyebrows furrowed and her jaw set—she refused to get out of the vehicle.

My colleague exited the truck and informed me, "She's mad that I brought her home." But I didn't need to be told—Carolina's disappointment and annoyance were apparent. She wanted to continue speeding down the roadways of Fieldpark, relishing a day away from the home, in the company of her two friends. Certainly not prepared to keep a smile plastered to her face in this situation, her squinted eyes and pouted lip were clear explanation; she was definitely and obviously annoyed. No high-fives here.

The much more verbal and communicative Missy was not immune to disappointment either. One afternoon, Glenda was hanging out in the kitchen, washing dishes and chatting with Missy. I heard a minor increase in the decibel level of the conversation and, when I walked in, Glenda grinned slyly and said, "Hey, Missy—tell that story to Sarah," then looked at me and winked.

Missy began, "My aunt let me borrow her necklace. When I was taking it off, it broke. I didn't do it on purpose. But my aunt said, 'I'm very mad at you BECAUSE YOU BROKE IT!'"

Apparently, as Glenda was already aware, every time Missy related that particular tale, when she reached the climactic plot point of the narration, she would scream just like her aunt had done. Glenda thought Missy's storytelling style was pretty amusing and continued to wink and smile at me behind her back.

I viewed the story, though, as a terrible memory for Missy where she felt that she had been reprimanded harshly, unjustly, and a bit frighteningly. The event was so significant to her that she remembered, clearly, not only her aunt's words, but the unfairly exaggerated vocal volume. I ignored Glenda and told Missy, "Oh, you must have felt so bad." I didn't know what else to say. But, from then on, I tried to praise Missy a little more often for cleaning or tidying, just to let her know that she was doing good things. And I spoke to her with respect.

Even Angeline, with all her giddy playfulness, had the ability to feel rotten. Inhabitants of the home loved hanging out in the garage, set up as a makeshift entertainment area. There was a well-used, faded rug in the center of the cement floor, partially hidden under a worn-out brown couch and a scratched and beverage-cup-ringed coffee table. To the side of the couch was Angeline's cherished record player. Next to the turntable, there was a small stack of records, most importantly, the two records that Angeline played daily. One album had a portrait on the cover of five or six '80s-style band members. I don't know what the group was called or their musical genre, but with their sculpted and sprayed bleached-blonde hair standing straight up over black, pseudo-leather outfits with shoulder pads and puffy pants, they looked like a Flock of Seagulls knock-off.

The other music Angeline played daily was The Knack's, "My Sharona." This record must have been a single, because I don't remember any more of The Knack's music materializing before or after this selection—just, "My Sharona" several times a day. I didn't mind. I had the personal habit of playing records at home with the L-shaped support bar lifted off the record and moved to the side, allowing Eurythmics or Thompson Twins to start again and again from the beginning after the end of side one. But Missy was usually annoyed by Angeline's limited musical variety and would complain, "Angeline plays, 'My *Ashrona*,' over and over! Why doesn't she play something else?"

When, one afternoon, all the residents were having a My Sharona Dance Party in the garage, Angeline was called into the house for a meeting. Several adults in suits were present, so I assumed the consultation was regarding Angeline's schooling. She was gone for a short time—maybe 20 minutes or half an hour. But the moment Angeline returned to the garage, she plopped down on the couch and started crying loud, heaving sobs. I reached out to touch her arm consolingly, but she snatched it away shouting, "No!" Respectfully, I obliged and left her alone.

However, when Angeline was able to calm down and habitually reach for the Flock of Seagulloids record, Missy complained, "I don't want to listen to that!" I definitely understood Missy's desire to break away from tradition, but I thought it was more important to give Angeline a little extra consideration on that occasion. I informed Missy, loudly enough for Angeline to overhear and emotionally benefit, "Angeline's having a bad day, so she gets to choose the music we'll listen to now." Being the subject of a meeting with lots of tie-wearing adults might have made Angeline feel powerless; I wanted to give her back a touch of that power. There wasn't anything more profound that I could actually do to help improve Angeline's spirits, but I hope that small gesture made her feel regarded, and, thus, a tiny bit better.

By just being themselves, the residents of the Fieldpark home, especially the girls with Down syndrome, taught me about compassion, human variety, and acceptance. I enjoyed the company of those girls immensely. They were amusing, emotionally diverse, and they filled me with joy. There was something about them that was attractive; they were magnets and my teenage enthusiasm was their metal. They made work unlike work and more like play.

For this reason, I always felt puzzled that the three of them were living full-time in this care home rather than with their own families. All of them could bathe, dress, use bathroom facilities, prepare meals, and clean up on their own. Missy, especially, was highly advanced; I imagine that she probably moved into her own apartment when she reached adulthood. What caused the families of those three young women to decide that they should not grow up at home?

I remembered seeing a little girl with Down syndrome, possibly two or three years old, in a stroller at the mall. She was tightly grasping one of those hand-held back massagers that looked like it could have come from a giant game of jacks—a cluster of four or five gold metal arms with a wooden ball on each end. The little girl was happily manipulating the figure, smiling at the shiny metal rods and smooth brown spheres. Occasionally, her mother would guide the toy to the little girl's back and rub her soft pink neck with it. The girl wouldn't let go of the toy, reaching over her own shoulder while her mother massaged, making both of them grin and giggle. She was the first baby with Down syndrome I had ever seen.

I looked down at that girl and couldn't help but smile. Her enjoyment of the world, and her mother's enjoyment of her were captivating. The two were sharing a bond that was so pure—it was love in its most basic form. I was envious of the mother who had been blessed with such a perfectly angelic little girl.

While I remained a silent bystander to cherubic beauty, the obvious suddenly came to the forefront of my mind—Missy, Angeline, and Carolina were babies once. They were tiny and smiling and cuddly, and they thought things were shiny and smooth. But were they appreciated in their miniature states? Did they provoke grins from envious bystanders who caught their eyes? Were their cheeks pinched, their tummies tickled, their toes kissed? Were they entertained? Were they cherished? Or had they always lived in a residential care facility? Or an institution? This little girl at the mall was on an outing with her mommy, not residing in a care home, not a tenant, but a family member, living with someone who loved her. Mother and daughter were out and about, appreciating life and each other. The small child was being valued for the natural gift she gave her mother—childish joy. Both were happy. If I could have, I'd have picked up the girl and taken some of that happiness with me.

That child, in one brief moment at the mall, gave me my first glimpse of the future—I wanted to hold a little baby with Down syndrome in my arms.

Chapter 5:

Loss

Time passed by, life went on, and I grew up. The end of high school brought the beginning of college and my decision to concentrate on higher learning. I was devastated to have to leave the care homes. I instantly missed the children and regretted my choice to leave. The following Christmas, I paid a visit and brought small gifts over for all the Fieldpark residents. However, when I rang the bell, Hari answered the door and informed me that everyone was away for the day—there was no one there for me to see. I gave him the gifts to pass out on my behalf and left. Although I sent yearly Christmas cards to the home, that was the last time I ever stood on that doorstep.

For the past 20 years, since I stopped working at both homes, I have thought about those children and young adults over and over again. Shortly after I left, my mom showed me an article in our local newspaper which stated that the homes had been closed. Having read the article, I drove past the home where Les and Christopher had lived, and saw that the structure was no longer a place of business—just a regular single-family residence. I can't remember how to get to the Fieldpark home.

I regularly dream about those kids. In the dreams, I suddenly see one of them in a crowded public place, like a store or classroom. When I hear the child's name or otherwise discover their identity, I start heaving sobs of relief that my old friend is still alive. Underneath the ecstatic relief lurks a pervasive sadness that the child no longer remembers me.

I would give anything to know where those children are now. Are they living with their families? Are they in other care homes? So many years have gone by—they would be so different. Jeffrey would be 34. Missy would be 38. Like Les, some of the children from the Westview home might be gone. I hope with all my heart that they are alive and thriving and, most of all, that they are loved, if not by a parent, then at least a worker who cares enough about them to give them secret hugs filled with love. They all deserve love.

When I was 18, I was interviewed by a USC student who was doing a class research project about euthanasia. Knowing where I worked, he wanted to interview me about my opinions on his thesis. He asked me several questions, but the gist of his line of inquiry was, as he finally stated succinctly, "Children like the ones you work with don't benefit the world at all, and their lives have no meaning. When the only thing keeping a severely disabled child alive is the fact that they're being fed, why not just stop feeding them and let them die?"

I responded, "You'd die, too, if you stopped eating. Eating keeps everyone alive." Talking to this interviewer about a point of view so completely opposed to mine immediately put me on the defensive. He was telling me that some of the people I loved most in the world deserved to be dead. How would Les' parents have reacted to the same line of questions?

Almost ignoring my bluntly sarcastic response, he went on, "But people like that—they serve no purpose."

I tried to inform him of his misunderstanding: "They're living beings. When I hold them, I feel their warmth, and when I talk to them, I can tell that they're at peace. One boy, Les, used to look up at me and coo when I held him. I could tell that he loved me, and I loved him. What better purpose is there than that?"

The USC student's immediate retort was, "What was his name? Less? How ironic that his name was 'Less' when that's exactly what his life was."

It didn't matter what I said; this guy didn't get it, and he never would. That guy, as a person, was insignificant to me, but his opinion was of vital importance. His opinion on the value of life was 100% polar to my grain, and he was potentially going to publish said opinions in scholarly texts, spreading his word, which already seemed to be a widely held opinion. I was glad when he and his opinions left my house; I do appreciate him, however, for bringing the notion of life's meaning to the forefront of my mind. It has remained there.

I've heard, many times, people talk about that concept: the meaning of life. "What is the meaning of life?" "Without purpose, what meaning does life have?" My response: What do you mean by *meaning*? Is it the benefit to oneself? Or the benefit to others? The benefit to society? Or is one's meaning in the world related to the accomplishment of their goals? Or is it relationships and love? Or is it importance?

Since my questions have largely gone unanswered, and since the definition of *meaning of life* seems to be pretty loose and poetic anyway, I've made my own definition: Life's meaning is related to the importance that one's own life has, and every single human life has importance. I challenge anyone to argue that the lives of the children at Bernadette's homes have—or had—no importance. They directed me down the numerous paths I came upon after meeting them. They made me who I am now. What's more important than guiding and shaping a life?

From the beginning of my relationship with these beautiful children at the home, no outsider could fully grasp my soulful connection, my heart's yearning to be near this particular population of human beings. My boyfriend didn't want to visit me at work because the kids grossed him out. When Les died, to quell my tearful grief, my best friend in the halls at our high school patted me on the back and said, "You'll be fine," and sprinted off to class. In fact, many insiders didn't understand my feelings too well, either. My teenage coworker at the home said once, with frightening nonchalance, "I can't stand Nikki. Which kid do you hate most?" Except for Bernadette and Debbie, I felt like I was the only person in the world who didn't just, coincidentally, share the earth with these children but wanted to and cherished being near them.

I would give anything to be near them just one more time.

Chapter 6:

Lessons

I was born in an ideal town for raising a child, Robinson Hills, California. It's not a bustling business district with high rises and the danger of being mowed down by distracted businessmen in their BMWs at every corner. But Robinson Hills also isn't the boonies; we don't have a whole lot, but we do have a choice of movie theaters and restaurants. We had a drive-in when I was growing up. I miss that drive-in. I loved going there with my family, back when I thought the actors were inside the screen performing the movies, climbing around within a thin, vertical stage. Now that drive-in is a Marshall's. But Robinson Hills is still pretty much the way it was then: small but welcoming, friendly but quiet—kind of how I was as a kid.

I was a thin, freckled, redheaded, shy little girl who was eager to please. My mom often tells me, "When I had your brother, he always screamed and cried at bedtime. When you came along, I thought, 'Oh, here we go again.' But at night, you would just say [in Mom's exaggerated, good-little-girl tone], 'Oh, Mother, may I go to bed now, please?' It was such a pleasure!" The only thing I liked better than Mom tucking me into bed at night was falling asleep with my head on her stomach, groggily listening to her tummy gurgles while she stroked my red hair.

Dad was my hero. He held onto my bike when I was six years old and ran by my side until I was able to pedal on my own. He continued to run behind me, yelling, "You're doing it! You're riding your bike!" I remember kids running out of their houses, sprinting by my side, cheering and shouting, "Keep pedaling! Keep pedaling!" Dad was very proud of me that day and, as always, I could tell.

My older brother was my best friend. When we were about seven and 10 years old, he and I were playing blind man's bluff together on our cul-de-sac one afternoon; we had no idea how to play, really, but the title made it sound like a fun game. In our version, we both closed our eyes and ran around trying, blindly, to tag each other. We only ended up running into each other full-speed, skidding across the street, asphalt body-surfing in duo. We both burst into tears, not because of our own injuries, but me bawling because he was hurt, and vice versa.

I had friends on our cul-de-sac and at school, but I enjoyed nothing more than spending time with my family. I loved my parents and big brother, and felt most comfortable with them. Thanks to my family, I look back and consider my childhood ideal.

Aside from Spanish dancing, Mom had, over numerous summers, signed me up for varied interesting and creative classes organized by the parks and recreation center in our area. I went to animation class, guitar class, acting class, folk dancing class, and sign language class, among about a bazillion other classes.

When I was a junior in high school and trying to decide what my major would be in college, Mom must have remembered those community classes, especially my absolute favorite, American Sign Language. When I told her I was undecided about a future course of study, she suggested offhandedly, "Well, Nann's daughter, Julie, is a sign language interpreter."

A mental slide show of my childhood lessons in and resulting obsession with ASL flashed before me. My response to Mom was a shouted, wide-eyed, "Of course!" The idea of studying sign language seemed like I had just discovered life's ultimate truth. I had always loved languages, and ASL was my preferred non-English enthrallment. Sign language was my instant and permanent first choice of higher-learning path. I was one of those rare kids who knew exactly what they wanted to do after high school and actually did it.

I studied American Sign Language at a local community college and got an associate's degree in interpreting for the deaf, a fulfilling and educational profession that I've enjoyed thoroughly. When I first began my studies, my goal was to teach sign language to people with developmental disabilities. That didn't happen, though. No one had ever heard of the concept, and I was young, shy, and didn't know how to pursue it myself. The ASL interpreting program guided me toward interpreting for typical deaf folks, and, with a minor twinge of disappointment, I willingly and happily went along that road.

My entrance into college life was made difficult by the fact that, the day after I graduated from high school, my mom announced that she was moving out. During my first college semester, my mother asked for a divorce from my dad. At 18, considered an adult, I probably should have taken the divorce better. But 18 years was a long time to think I had a closer-than-the-Brady-Bunch family; suddenly having that union torn apart was a devastating blow to my sense of reality. Family vacations, Christmas mornings, movie nights, and a feeling of security in the knowledge that I had a home to go to were all ripped out from under me. My brother dealt with the situation by spending his time with Debbie at their apartment in Los Angeles. I hardly saw him or talked to him for months. Personally, my home-base for layovers between college classes and work or over the weekends vanished, leaving me, far too suddenly after high school graduation, with no place to call home. My family unit disappeared, exploding in a glittery puff of Brady Bunch sequins, leaving only my Married with Children fury. College became the place where I finally did some angry, teenage rebelling, including dating and desperately hanging on to all the wrong guys in a useless attempt to get a family back into place.

Transition into adult life was an unexpected and angry shove from the nest with an inability to fly; however, I taught myself to flap my wings and began life as an adult on my own. My emotional recovery after the divorce was a long trek, but I made it out of that dark cave and back into the light, as did my heartbroken dad and confused mom. Dad found a great new wife, Bea, who loves the heck out of him. Mom eventually got remarried to Rob, a nature lover who takes her bird watching and camping like she had always wanted. I couldn't seem to ever bond with Rob personally, but Mom was happy—that was the important part. As I told Dad, for a rotten thing like divorce, it actually all turned out pretty nicely in the end.

Even now when I dream, however, I'm about 18 years old and in my old bedroom, my brother in his, and my parents are together, still in their room right down the hall.

* * *

The sign language path led me to postsecondary ASL interpreting. Shortly after I got my degree in Sign Language Interpreting, I happened to run into a young deaf person I knew from college. The student was attending a community college in southern California and needed a sign language interpreter. This was in the early 1990s; the Americans with Disabilities act was quite new, and many educational establishments were having a hard time finding the now-legally-mandated sign language interpreters. This student's class had no interpreter, so the unfortunate deaf person would sit for three hours each day with no idea what was being discussed. Furthermore, the class he was taking was Korean Language 101. I was young, enthusiastic, and poor. Since I had my own place now, a real, adult-type job was a necessity. I called the director of the college's Student Resources Center and asked for the interpreter job. They were thrilled to hear from me and hired me without ever meeting me.

The next thing I knew, I was sitting at the front of a college-level Korean class failing miserably at interpreting the professor's instruction. I hardly knew what to do with a class conducted in a language I couldn't understand and a student who constantly flirted with me and told inappropriate jokes. But I stuck with it and learned.

As the years progressed, I became the first staff interpreter at that school. After years of hard work and improvement, I found myself coordinating the schedules for 10 hourly sign language interpreters and 20 deaf college students. I felt that I had accomplished something important. An added and vital bonus was that the interpreters became some of the best friends I'd ever had; they remain so.

For one of my deaf-student-services improvement schemes at the college, I needed to borrow recording equipment to make an interpreter training video, so I headed to the college's Media Center. I was assisted there by a very friendly, very funny, and very handsome man, Walter. I found myself needing to go back to the Media Center for more and more reasons—to return equipment, to borrow it again because I'd returned it too soon, then to re-return it. I had a serious crush.

After weeks of Media Center visits—Walter now lovingly calls it "stalking"—he had finally received enough of my ask-me-out vibes. He called me at my office.

"Hello?"

"Hi, is Sarah there?"

[Flutter, flutter] "Yes, this is Sarah."

"This is Walter from the Media Center."

[I already knew that.] "Oh, really? Hey, how's it going?"

"Well, I was planning on seeing *Drop Dead Gorgeous* with a few friends of mine on Friday and I was wondering if you would be interested in accompanying me."

I was. But I couldn't. Debbie and my brother had been married for six years, and they were about to give birth to my first nephew. Friday was the night before Deb's baby shower, and I was the hostess. I would need to spend the evening tying ribbons on party favors and wrapping shower-game prizes.

"Ew...I'm busy on Friday night. I'm sorry, I'd really like to, but I just can't."

When Walter relates this story, he explains that this was when he said to himself, "Oh, great. Now it's going to be like every other girl I ask out who doesn't actually want to go out. 'Then how about Saturday?' 'No, I'm washing my hair on Saturday.' 'Then how about Sunday?' 'No, I'm getting my nails done on Sunday.' Rather than just telling me she's not interested, I'm going to look like an idiot. Terrific."

But then I continued the explanation. "I'm hosting my sister-in-law's baby shower on Saturday and I need to prepare. I'm way too busy to go out the night before. But what are you doing on Sunday?"

He responded, "I'm going out with you?" I found that response adorable, and he appreciated my enthusiastic interest.

Our plan was that he would pick me up at my apartment at 1:00 and we would walk to the nearby movie theater to see what was playing. But when Sunday arrived, I awoke with a major headache which followed me around all morning. Walter arrived at 1:00 and I answered the door looking as cute as possible but feeling like heck.

Now for Walter's account. He looked at the pained expression on my face and thought, "Here we go again. I came to get her, but she's going to cancel out. Now I'm going to have to ask for a bunch of alternative dates and look like an idiot."

But what I ended up saying was, "Walter, I hate to do this, but I have a terrible headache. Is it ok if we cancel going out to a movie? I'd feel better just walking to Blockbuster, renting a couple of movies, and chilling on the couch."

That's when Walter says he first started falling in love. I was interested in him and let it be known. I, however, took a little longer to come around and make an exit at love's off-ramp. A crush was one thing, but *love* was another. Having been famous for making bad decisions, especially after my parents' divorce, I hadn't had the best of luck with men. But during our two-week winter break, Walter and I spent every moment together getting to know each other. I already knew he was funny and smart, but I got to see his amazing giving nature. Not only was he nurturing and caring with me, but he helped whenever possible with strangers. In public, if he ever saw someone in need of a little assistance, he would be the first one there to lend a hand. If a woman at the grocery store had a lot of bags in her cart, he would ask if she needed help loading her car. If he saw a man carrying a table into a house, Walter would pull the car over, jump out, and grab a corner. That's when I decided I really did love the guy.

Three months later, I woke up to find a path of long-stemmed roses leading from the hallway to the front door. Each rose had a note next to it with a message: "You are beautiful." "You are smart." "You are funny." "You are talented." "I want to spend the rest of my life with you." Then, on a pink construction-paper heart, "Sarah, will you marry me?"

I was late to work that day.

Walter and I were engaged for a year and a half, and we were married on January 17. I was 30 and he was 37.

We lived for a little while in my Mar Vista apartment. As it was in a rent controlled area, we were able to save up money to purchase a place of our own. Eventually, we bought a nice little house in El Segundo. We were happy to have found a home in our price range and in line with our requirements of three bedrooms, a back yard, and a fireplace. However, we always knew it would be a starter house. It was right next to the freeway—we could see the blue garage door of our house as we sped down the 405. Directly across the freeway from us were the low-income housing projects where we would, at least weekly, see helicopters flying over at night, shining their lights down searching for someone or something I didn't want to know about. And the neighborhood elementary school where our new daughter, Heidi, would eventually go was directly across the street from the helicopter projects; known drug dealers were recruiting new customers at that school, aptly named "Leary Elementary". But every single neighbor on our street—properly labeled Paradise Avenue—was friendly and warm, and we all took care of each other with parties and play-dates.

Immediately after Heidi's birth, Walter and I went through what we can look back on and call *a bad patch*. Walter was working at the college at night and at a coffee shop in the morning to keep up with monthly mortgage payments. I was working full-time, as well as taking care of Heidi in the evenings while Walter was at work. Walter and I hardly ever saw each other, and when we were together, he wanted to only sleep. I felt left all alone, and he felt that his needs weren't being met. Before much time had passed, we had mastered the art of the snarky side comment and the stink-eye glare. We began marriage counseling, and I told the therapist that I had become indifferent about the marriage.

One evening when we were actually sitting peacefully together on the couch, we saw a Wanda Sykes stand-up comedy routine. She was talking about the banality of gay marriage and said the biggest threat to the institution of marriage was not homosexual unions; "The biggest threat to marriage is divorce."

We were both struck strongly by that comment. When he was 11, Walter's parents divorced after several years of snarky stink-eyes, and my parents divorced as suddenly as an earthquake. For whatever reason, both couples thought breaking up their marriages was more important than trying to make the unions succeed, and Walter and I both suffered permanent psychological repercussions.

We decided then, marriage is hard and requires work. We won't always agree, but we will always be a family. And we have Heidi. She is the rope that ties us together. As the world's most awesome daughter, she deserves our hard work. And as we are all a family and I would never divorce my daughter, I will also never divorce my husband. We're a unit, and we're in it for the duration.

Walter and I went to counseling with a new mindset and different goals. Personally, I blinked a couple of times, wiped the fuzziness away from my eyes, and took another look at my husband. I had married him because he was super funny, really cute, and very, very giving. Those qualities had not changed. I just needed to step out of my own postpartum stress and take a good look at the man I married. He was still cute.

And Heidi sure was a cute little baby. She had huge blue eyes and a tiny nose which always made her look, to me, like a little mouse. She smiled at anyone and everyone. She was a fairly easy child, but I was grateful to Bernadette and the work I had done in my youth at her homes. Taking care of six severely disabled children taught me two things. First, I learned to change a diaper at top speed. Having up to six large and fully dependent children to take care of meant a lot of possibilities per day for soiled Pampers and not much time for cuddly bonding while changing. And, apparently, changing a diaper is like riding a bike—you never forget how. So when Heidi appeared 15 years later, I was able to wipe her off and switch her up like an Indy 500 pit crew chief.

The second thing Bernadette's home, and Bernadette specifically, taught me is that children cry for a reason. One afternoon, Bernadette and I stood at Manny's crib while I helped her change his clothes. He had a little fever and some diarrhea, so I saw the visible evidence that he was sick. But then he started to cry. I had never heard him talk, move with purpose, or make a facial expression. But when he cried, I saw tears run down his face.

Bernadette said, "It breaks my heart when he cries, because it has to mean he's in pain." Manny probably had a horrible stomach ache, and agony broke through the expressionlessness. Thankfully, I held on to that memory when Heidi was born. Babies don't necessarily have to be colicky to cry for hours into the night. When Heidi was two days old and my milk hadn't come in yet, she cried for hours and hours, and I knew the only thing I could do was hold her to insufficiently comfort her. If she was sick or teething and crying as a result, I would do the same. Sometimes I would feed her, change her, hold her, burp her, rock her, and never figure out what was making her cry. But I never once wanted to shake her and shout at her to shut the heck up. I didn't need to figure out what was making her cry. I would remember Manny and think, "Maybe she has a stomach ache," or some other malady that hadn't been made apparent. Then I'd rub her tummy a bit and say, "I know, baby. You're so sad." The absence of parental panic on my end probably helped her relax, and she would generally stop crying. If she didn't stop, I would just hold her knowing that, like Manny, she had her reasons.

Chapter 7:

Path

House and family in new-and-improved working order, on Paradise Avenue for 4 years and with Heidi for two, life was feeling pretty close to perfect. But after 14 years of working in the sign language profession, I realized that I'd been missing the connection I once shared with the disabled community, especially people with Down syndrome. Although he already knew of my personal infatuation with the developmentally disabled, I told Walter about my childhood musings regarding adoption and my deep affection for people with Down syndrome.

"We have such a great family—why not share it with someone? There are babies out there who some people might not necessarily want to adopt, like babies born with disabilities—but we could adopt a baby like that. And I've always loved Down syndrome. I'd really like us to consider adopting a child with Down syndrome."

And Walter, bless his big ol' heart, actually did take the time to consider my idea. After much discussion about the topic, and about our mutual desire to do some greater good during our time here on earth, Walter finally announced, "Let's go for it."

Although we were both excited by the idea, we didn't want to jump hastily into something as huge as bringing a new child into our home. We continued to talk about the pros and cons of adoption for several more months and just take the idea a little slowly before taking any actual steps toward adoption.

As a precursor to action, we thought it was a good time to begin letting our parents in on our plan. Adoption might seem strange to them since Walter and I have no infertility issues. Also, adopting a baby with special needs could be a concept they'd want to ask questions about and get a mental handle on. The latter ended up being true—very true.

I told my mom first. Sitting on her couch in the living room of the house where I grew up, I reminded her of the love and connection I've always had with people who have Down syndrome, and I told her we'd decided to adopt just such a wonderful child.

In response, my mom asked me some superficial questions about our plan—how would we find a baby and how much would it cost? Although her questions were very basic, I could tell she was concerned. Her voice had the energy of overt bubbliness that it tended to acquire when she was uncomfortable with a situation.

I was right. The next day, she sent me a long email listing all of her concerns about a child with Down syndrome—expenses, possible medical problems, time taken away from Heidi, shortened life span— all of which I allayed as much as possible in my emailed response— we have insurance, we will go through any necessary surgeries with a new baby just as we would with any child, we'll have special time allotted for Heidi, medical advances have lengthened the expected life span of those with Down syndrome. It was a very matter-of-fact email exchange full of information simply to quell fears.

But then, I began to wonder—Mom was the first parent I told, very open-minded and welcoming of difference and disability, and she didn't react to the news positively at all. If I brought a disabled grandchild into her home, would she still welcome the addition as she had Heidi? And as she was always so accepting of people with disabilities, how would other, more inexperienced relatives react to a child with Down syndrome? Would they behave awkwardly with the new baby? Would they want to bond with their new grandchild? Would my new son or daughter have any grandparents to bond with?

By way of asking my mom all of these questions, I sent her another email,

"When we go to pick up our new baby, will you go with us?"

Her brief response told me I had nothing to fear for my future child's grandparently relations:

"I wouldn't miss it for the world."

I felt better. Inspired but still on guard, next was to inform my father.

I wasn't looking forward to telling him. Rather than composing lengthy emails listing comprehensive concerns, Dad tends to quietly fret, especially in regard to me, my welfare, and my decisions. I chose to give Dad a brief synopsis of our plan during one of our lunch visits at his house.

Over diet 7-Ups in his tastefully-decorated living room, I began.

"Dad, I wanted to talk to you about something."

He tentatively smiled and replied with a worried chuckle, "Heh…yes?"

I softened the introduction of the concept with, "I wanted to let you know that Walter and I are planning on adopting a baby."

"Okay," he said with another nervous snicker.

Taking a deep breath, I summoned up the courage and quickly reeled off, "We specifically want a baby with Down syndrome."

"Oh," he uttered, "You always did like those children you worked with." He seemed to accept the notion, and took it upon himself to conclude the conversation with, "Okay, I trust your decision."

Really, that's all I can remember about the exchange. Dad didn't have much to say about our plan or have much of a reaction to our decision. But I had done my part; I had mustered up the courage to tell my father. I left him alone to silently worry.

The next prospective grandparent to inform was Walter's mom, Minnie.

Now, Minnie—she's quite a personality. I love her dearly, but that love came from months of learning just what kind of a person she really is. When Walter and I were dating and I first met his mother, she presented herself, I have come to learn, the way she usually does with new acquaintances. She always conducted herself very politely, but after a few minutes of conversation, she revealed her true self: opinionated, self-righteous, and just plain loud. And lots of swearing. It's not that I'm a prude—I can throw a well-aimed F-bomb when necessary. I had just never heard so much lavatory language from someone's mother. Definitely never from my own mom. My initiation into Walter's family was a culture shock of sorts, especially when his brother, Keith, came over to meet me as well. Between Keith and Minnie, I had never heard so many varied and colorful curse-words tossed about with such casual nonchalance before.

But over time, along with the realization that Keith is one of my favorite people, I came to learn that not every maternal figure is like mine. In fact, a cursing, commiserating mother-in-law can be a lot of fun. After making it through the initial shock of her rough exterior, I found the fluffy center. The woman's a gem, and I love her dearly. She's funny, welcoming, a pleasure to spend time with, a good conversationalist, and one incredible effing grandma.

When the time came to tell Minnie about our adoption plan, I had an idea of the reaction we would get from her. As an opinionated woman, I knew we weren't going to have to wonder what her thoughts were. She would let us know.

Sitting in her condo, Walter and I on the floor, Heidi and GrandMinnie snuggling in a burgundy recliner, I began: "Walter and I wanted to tell you what we're in the process of doing. We are trying to adopt a baby."

"Oh, that's a great idea," she began. "You're such a great family. You're not having trouble getting pregnant, are you? No? Oh, that's good. There are so many children out there that need homes."

Before she got too excited, I interrupted to tell her the real point.

"We specifically want to adopt a baby with Down syndrome."

"Why would you do that?" was her immediate response. *Here it comes*, I thought. And then the flood of aforementioned opinions presented itself.

"Heidi is very intelligent. She deserves to have a sibling who is her equal. It's unfair to her to intentionally bring in a child who will never be her equal. And the child is going to grow up having other kids make fun of him at school. That's going to be so heartbreaking. And you're going to have extra medical expenses—money is already tight for you, now. And when you're gone, Heidi is going to have the burden of taking care of him. It's cruel to give her that type of lifelong burden. And...."

I quietly listened, nodded, and uh-huhed with each comment, but as she wasn't pausing between each new concern, I didn't respond. However, as she vented, I simply told myself, "She just doesn't know about Down syndrome. Once she meets the baby, she's going to fall in love." I was so certain of Minnie's goodness and her adoration of her grandchildren that her diatribe bounced off me like so many swear words. I knew she'd come around. I checked her name off the list.

The last grandparent to tell was Walter's dad, Danny. We don't see much of Danny, as he lives in another state. But more than the distance, Walter and Danny's personal history keeps them from getting as close as they could. Danny felt that his five children needed to be trained by him to know who the boss in the family was, and the boss was definitely Danny. His methods of asserting his alpha status ranged from a hard rap on the knuckles with the handle of a knife at dinner, to a screaming, drunken chase around the house wielding a leather belt studded with large brass rings. Walter once dodged the belt in time to let it land on the closet instead of his back, leaving a brass-ring shaped impression in the white-painted surface of the door.

Not only was Danny physically abusing his children, but he had affair after affair, emotionally abusing his wife. Minnie silently retaliated with passive-aggressive creativity, such as by taking his brand-new Italian suit out of the closet, snipping every other stitch, and replacing it on the hanger. Shortly after leaving the house and heading to a business meeting, his clothes fell apart.

Since Danny and Walter had a difficult, issue-riddled relationship when Walter was a child, the two of them have had a strained relationship now that they're both adults. However, every year, Danny volunteered at the Special Olympics in southern California, running a booth where he let athletes paint and decorate their own T-shirts, and Walter and I always looked forward to assisting Danny in this annual event. We enjoyed participating in the Special Olympics and meeting the athletes and their families; the day's visit with Danny made Walter feel like a dutiful son's visitation responsibilities were sufficiently scratched off the list for the year.

Standing with Danny under the canopy of his shirt-painting booth, a line of developmentally disabled children and adults enjoying sequins and glitter-glue, I decided to give him the news that we were going through the process of adopting a baby with Down syndrome.

His response puzzled me. With a completely expressionless face, he looked me straight in the eye and asked,

"What's the *magic* of Down syndrome?" I noted clearly the sarcasm in his voice, as well as the nostrils-flared, lips-pressed-together expression, identical to the one Walter puts on when he expects the statement he's just made to be challenged.

I stammered momentarily, desperately resisting the urge to respond, "They can fly." I ended up babbling something about my life-long love of Down syndrome before he was called away to tend to Sharpies and puff paint. We never spoke of the situation again.

Informing all of the parents was, thus, taken care of.

Chapter 8:

Questions

Walter was open and willing to talk about adoption, but he was somewhat silent on the specific issue of Down syndrome. There didn't seem to be a problem, but in a situation as serious as this one, I had to be sure. I didn't want to embark on the process of adopting a disabled child without the full support of my husband. If Walter wasn't in complete mental union with me, an adoption absolutely could not happen. Bringing an unwanted child into the house would cause a huge fault to develop within our family, unfair to everyone involved, including the adopted child, and not good at all for the new and improved Cavilry union. I thought I'd better check in and make sure we were in agreement completely, not just about adopting a child in general, but about adopting a child with Down syndrome. So, over dinner one weekend evening, I initiated a little conversation.

"Honey, can we talk?"

"Oh, no," he replied with mock concern, "What did I do now?"

I laughed at the familiar joke, "Nothing bad. I just want to talk about the adoption. Is now a good time?"

"Sure. What's on your mind?"

"Is there anything about adopting that's concerning you at all?"

"Well…" he paused.

There was.

Now it was my turn to be concerned, and I certainly wasn't joking. I felt blood rush to my face in a worry-induced mini-panic. Were my dreams of holding a child with Down syndrome in my arms to remain unrealized? The dream of adopting a baby with Down syndrome was mine, not his, and I had to accept the reality that he might not want to go through with the plan that I had initiated.

I breathed deeply and braced myself to accept disappointment with mature understanding. "Tell me what's concerning you."

"Well," he began again, "Heidi is so important to me. I'm afraid of a new baby taking up all of our time so we can't give Heidi one-on-one attention anymore."

I wondered what his apprehensions about Down syndrome were, but I addressed this worry about Heidi first. "With a new baby in the house, we would definitely need to make sure to keep having family time on the weekends, but to also have special Mommy- or Daddy-alone-time—maybe once a month—with Heidi."

Walter replied, simply, "That's a great idea. I like that."

But I needed to know what it was about Down syndrome that was making him wary of adoption. After a too-long pause, I braced myself again and reworded the previous question. "Is there anything about adopting a baby with Down syndrome that's worrying you?"

Without faltering, he smiled and stated, in a wonderfully matter-of-fact manner, "Not at all. I'm in total support of adopting a baby with Down syndrome."

I breathed a huge sigh of relief—audibly. "Phew!"

Walter laughed. "We have a great family, and we should share it with someone who needs us. I don't see the reason to bring more children into the world when there are already kids that need homes."

We were officially on the same page, and I was so grateful to him for his willing openness to join me on this undertaking. Now, it was time to really get started with this adoption.

* * *

I had no idea how to find a baby to adopt, so I began the easy way—I did a Google search for "Down syndrome adoption".

At the top of the results page, I found the National Down Syndrome Adoption Network. On that site, I filled out a detailed application and turned it in, thus adding our name to a list of families wanting to adopt American children with Down syndrome. I learned that there are generally around 200 families on that list, families that either already have a child with Down syndrome and crave a second, or that have past experiences like mine and want Down syndrome in their daily lives. But since NDSAN gets an average of five calls each week regarding babies in need of placement, we were called by Robin, coordinator of the adoption program, after only about a month on the list.

When I received her call on my cell phone, I was with Walter and Heidi waiting to be seated at Johnny Rockets on the 3rd Street Promenade in Santa Monica with our long-time friends, Atusa and Sam. The couple had been kept up to date on how much I wanted a child with Down syndrome and about our plan to adopt. So, when my phone rang with an incoming call from out of state, Atusa and Sam understood my excitement. I excused myself, headed for an alcove next to a neighboring clothing store, and answered my phone with anticipation.

"Hello?"

"Good evening. May I speak to Sarah?"

"This is Sarah!" I answered with a bit too much energy. I was already forming an expanded family unit in my imagination. Would we, so soon, have a new child? Nervous excitement made my stomach feel like a bouncy castle at a birthday party.

Robin said the phrase I'd been waiting to hear: "There's a child with Down syndrome who has been born in Nevada. Are you interested in pursuing adoption?"

I enthusiastically replied, "Absolutely."

"Great," the coordinator replied. "Is your home study complete?"

The castle deflated. I had never heard of a home study before, and the inclusion of the word *study* in the phrase didn't sound like something I could gather up in a few minutes and send off.

Indeed, it wasn't. When I ignorantly queried, "What's a home study?" I was informed that I would need to find an adoption agency to interview us and collect information on our home and family. Robin promised to see if the home study could be completed after the adoption process was begun.

However, before she could get the answer for me, I received a follow-up call from Robin a day later stating that the situation with the baby from Nevada "...has been resolved." I wasn't sure what that meant and felt I shouldn't pry. But as a result, we were given time to properly complete a home study, which I had been told could take several months. That interchange forced me to settle into a more patient frame of mind. The adoption was not going to be immediate, or so easy.

Robin gave me the contact information for West Coast Adoptions, the agency she regularly recommended to prospective Californian parents wishing to adopt. She referred me to Phyllis, a very nice woman who would pair our family up with a social worker to assist us in completing the home study.

As soon as Robin gave me the phone number, I called Phyllis, who then instructed me to make an appointment with a social worker named Eliza, which I also did immediately.

In addition, Phyllis scheduled us to attend a series of adoption workshops. The workshops would be two hours each and would take place once a week for a month. To attend these evening workshops, Walter would have to take time off from his 1:00 PM to 10:00 PM job, but the accrued absences were worth it to both of us—we were willing to do whatever we were expected to so that we could see this home study process to completion. Personally, I envisioned that little child, the tiny version of Missy, Angeline, or Carolina, cradling that sweet little baby in my arms, looking into her eyes and watching her grow, and looked forward to completing the work required to meet that glorious goal. And as far as the workshops themselves were concerned, Walter and I both looked forward to the possibility of asking questions and learning more about the adoption process.

* * *

At the first workshop, we met with Phyllis and two other couples in a small room at the West Coast offices. Three love seats lined three of four walls in the cozy, closet-like meeting room. Walter and I sat in the center loveseat, Phyllis in a chair across from us, her back to the door, the other two couples seated on her right and left. Phyllis had provided us with water and cookies, which she placed on the coffee table in the center of the room. I felt a little bit out of place, as the two other sets of prospective parents were each on their second adoption. But Walter and I both took their veteranism as an opportunity to ask questions about their experiences and receive some guidance.

Phyllis was very easy to talk to, extremely informative, and compassionately understood our desire to adopt a child with Down syndrome. I was slightly concerned, however, that the other couples were both, visibly, quite annoyed with having to go through this workshop process. They scowled, rolled their eyes, and looked at each other with bobbing eyebrows, arms folded. Walter and I tried to lighten the tension with humorous banter, but the audience was only barely and occasionally receptive.

One of the fathers brought up the fact that he and his wife didn't like the personality and philosophies of their social worker; they wanted to know if they had to accept the worker they'd been assigned or if they could be matched with another. The negativity surrounding the social workers, the adoption process, and West Coast Adoptions, as it was presented by these two couples, made me wary. Their apparent annoyance prompted me to be bubbly and talkative, and Walter upped his charisma quotient slightly. We continued to do our best to diffuse the awkwardness.

In general, I'm a nervous person, as Walter likes to often remind me. So, at the time, I told myself that my emotional discomforts were due to my own innate ability to be afraid of the unknown. This was simply another instance of irrational worry—I let the complainy couples complain and, in between times, I asked questions. The workshops, in general, ended up being informative and beneficial for Walter and me.

* * *

I had wanted, for many years, to go back to school. I only had my associate's degree; the world of sign language interpreting had kept me from obtaining a higher education. Now, with a young daughter as well, I figured I was just too busy for study. And anyway, as I told a friend, "If I go to school, it will take me three years. I'll be 38 by then."

She responded, "Well, would you rather be 38 with a degree, or 38 without a degree?" So, it was around this time that I decided to take advantage of my relative youth and go back to school.

Therefore, in addition to organizing a home study and working 40 hours a week interpreting, I enrolled full-time in Idaho State University's distance education program.

Studying for a bachelor's degree over the internet sounded a bit cheesy, but I soon discovered that my degree would not be easily achieved. I found myself a student in four hardcore university classes, complete with online classroom discussions, lengthy term papers, and comprehensive final exams. I even developed a full-fledged nervous tick: a leg that would bob up and down, vibrating constantly whenever I sat, to the annoyance of anyone unfortunate enough to be in my vicinity during a lengthy attack. Schooling was tough, and weekend family-time had to be put on hold, but if I didn't do it then, I might never do it. I buckled down, and, in between work, child-raising, home-study tasks, and repetitive leg-motion strain, I crammed.

After the completion of the adoption workshops, we made an appointment to meet at our house with Eliza, the social worker who was assigned to our case. When Eliza arrived at our door, she appeared perfectly pleasant and personable. She was a young, upbeat woman with long, straight, dark hair hanging down to her shoulders, and comfortably casual jean shorts and white T-shirt. Eliza smiled and was talkative.

Despite her casual, relaxed appearance and manner, I was nervous. I had been warned by a friend from work who had adopted a boy with autism from West Coast that the home study process would be emotionally difficult. She told me that the social worker would be digging deep into our histories, unearthing issues that might be painful to talk about. In fact, my work friend informed me that the home study was the worst experience of her life; she was asked questions about every aspect of her life, past and present, and it made her feel, "like the worst person in the world." My hope was that she simply had skeletons in her closet and I didn't.

But I was still unaware of what Eliza's actual questions would be, and the uncertainty of the situation kept me on edge. Although I had nothing to hide, I was like an innocent child getting a surprise summons to the principal's office—what had I done wrong? When I told my fears to Walter, he had coached, "Just answer all of her questions honestly and you'll be fine." Of course I would do that, but I was still nervous about the unknown.

Eliza began our interview with taking some preliminary notes—how we met, our family religion, where we work. She gave us a long list of documents we needed to collect—birth certificates; forms from our doctors confirming our good health; letters from relatives, friends, and Heidi's preschool teacher; and she gave us pages and pages of questions about our family. Eliza instructed us to mail each piece of paperwork to her as we collected it, and she would compile the documents into a Cavilry-Family file at the main West Coast office.

Then, Eliza began the oral portion of the interview with her first question: "So, Walter, what was your childhood like?"

My heart jumped a bit. Had Eliza asked me the same question, I wouldn't have been concerned. Walter hadn't had such a great childhood, and I momentarily worried about those skeletons. Fortunately, that thought was fleeting—I took a deep breath and, as I often do, let my charismatic husband take charge.

Walter described his relationship with his parents: his father's alcoholism and physical abuse, his mother's passive aggression, their divorce, and his feelings of inadequacy. Eliza asked for additional specific points of clarification in response to each commentary, and Walter, in the end, seemed to have passed the test. My husband has a captivating quality, and listening to him talk will usually win anyone over—not that Eliza needed winning over, but it certainly couldn't hurt.

"Have you gone to therapy to deal with childhood issues?" Eliza questioned.

"Oh, definitely," Walter responded with matter-of-factness. "I've been in therapy, off and on, since I was 13."

"Good," Eliza replied with what seemed like relief. I kept that in mind.

Eliza then turned to look at me. "Now, Sarah. Tell me about your childhood."

In contrast with Walter's accounts of alcoholism and violence, my childhood was simple. I said so.

"My family was like the Brady Bunch. We loved each other, had family time together, went on vacations…I was happy."

"Wow, everything was perfect, huh?" Her response concerned me. It had a tinge of sarcasm.

I covered my possible error; "But my parents divorced when I was 18—and that devastated me."

She jumped on that information and asked, "Have you had any therapy for your issues concerning the divorce?"

Proudly, I told her, "Oh, yeah. I did."

"For how long?" she replied curtly.

I thought back on that time, nearly 20 years past, before answering honestly, "It was such a long time ago, but I guess it was about three months."

"Oh," she responded energetically, "that's not *nearly* enough to fully address the issues surrounding that event. You need to go to therapy and let your inner child have a voice. That's why you have weight issues."

I looked down over my muffin top and silently believed she was mistaken.

I'll be honest. I did gain weight after I got married. A lot of weight. About 75 pounds. But up until I was about 30, I was always thin or skinny. My weight gain was stereotypical marital laziness as was the initiation of Walter's paunch into our union. It had nothing to do with my parents' divorce.

Perhaps I looked confused, for Eliza concluded the topic with, "I won't approve this home study if you don't go to therapy."

Considering the best tactic to be just to do as she said, I responded, "Sure, I'll go to therapy. That's not a problem."

Eliza gave me the name and number of a therapist's office.

Satisfied, she moved on. "How is your marriage? Have you had any problems or issues?"

Walter and I looked at each other. Remembering his advice to just tell the truth, I did so. "We had a short period right after Heidi was born where we were at each other's throats all the time." With emphasis, I added, "We went to therapy for that, and we worked through a lot of issues. The therapy was good for us."

"When did that happen?"

"It was after we were married for about three years."

She seemed relieved. "Oh, that's typical. Lots of marriages go through that. But you're good now?"

Walter and I smiled at each other, and I responded to Eliza with a peppy, "Yes, we are."

"Good," she smiled back and moved on. "So, you specifically want to adopt a child with Down syndrome, right?

I answered with enthusiasm for the arrival of my favorite topic, "Yes, that's right!"

"Why Down syndrome? I mean, do you have any experience with Down syndrome kids?"

Although I told myself it was probably a resurfacing of nerves, the tone of her question made me feel challenged. Was there something wrong—something weird—about wanting to adopt a baby with Down syndrome? I felt the need to defend myself, but I answered calmly.

"Since I was 16 years old, I've worked with people who have different types of disabilities, including Down syndrome. I've always had a strong emotional connection with Down syndrome, and I think that, since we have a great family, I would like to share our family with a child who needs us."

I thought that was a pretty good answer, but she didn't react with the support and enthusiasm for our good deed that I had hoped for. Unblinking, she continued, "How do you feel about the possibility of raising a Down syndrome child?"

Hearing her repeatedly say, "Down syndrome child" rather than the widely preferred "child with Down syndrome"—letting the child come first rather than the label—let me know that she probably didn't have much experience with disabilities. However, picky PC phrasing aside, the question itself left me puzzled. I wasn't sure how to respond—I was going to have a new baby. Babies are exciting. I was excited. So, I continued to follow Walter's advice and just answer honestly.

"I feel good. I'm looking forward to it."

Eliza responded with a stern look and a slightly raised voice, "Well, raising a disabled child is hard! I don't think you should be so thrilled about it. I'd feel much better if you said you were terrified. That would be much more realistic."

I stared back at her, my eyes popping, my upper lip curled, my jaw slack, and my eyebrows raised, quite involuntarily dumbfounded. Initially, my only response was, "Oh, okay." But after a beat, I mustered up the brainpower to stammer, "But I think I have the experiences and the resources to get answers or help whenever I need to."

"Well, that's good, because it's going to be a lot of work." Leaving that topic to bounce around, pinball-style, in the bumpers of my head, Eliza continued. "Has Heidi had any exposure to Down syndrome kids?"

"Um, only briefly," I muttered, knowing it would be the wrong answer for Eliza. "Nothing in depth."

"Then," she ordered, "you need to find some way to have her meet Down's kids. Find a school or an organization or something. She needs to see what Down syndrome is like. She needs to be prepared. It's only fair to her."

At three years old, I didn't know why she needed to be prepped in this manner. Being so young, I believed that my daughter would come to think of a sibling with Down syndrome as being normal; I didn't want to bring a new child into the family after telling Heidi that her brother or sister was different from the rest of us *normals*. It didn't seem right to me, and doing so went against everything I believed.

Ever since the first time I encountered people with developmental disabilities, way back at the dance recital when I was a child, I had been taught that all people have their differences, and differences make people interesting, unique, and wonderful. I didn't want to tell my daughter that the baby we would adopt was going to be different, because I deeply believed that all people are different, and I had always done my best to implant that philosophy in Heidi's malleable brain. However, that was what Eliza wanted me to do—to take Heidi to look at some Down syndromes, live and in person. And Eliza had the power to accept or reject us as a potential adoptive family. So, feeling trapped, meekly, without asserting my beliefs, I nodded and muttered, "Okay."

The conclusion of the interview mercifully arriving, Eliza said, "Well, I guess that's about it. I'll need to make an appointment to come back and interview your daughter."

Eliza assured us that she would call again. Collecting her paperwork, she handed us some pre-addressed envelopes to send her the documents and letters as we gathered them. Walter and I showed her to the front door, waved goodbye, and that was that.

Alone again, Walter and I exhaled and hugged, the first meeting done. Then I immediately called Eliza's referral therapist's office.

* * *

Two weeks later, I called Eliza. I needed to ask her a technical question about some paperwork I was filling out. When she answered the phone, she gave me the answer I needed, and then went on to say, "I haven't received a letter from your therapist yet."

I was confused. I thought I had to go to therapy for a while, long enough to work through all the difficult childhood issues revolving my parents' divorce which might be hanging on and giving me love handles. But Eliza wanted a letter immediately. So I asked for clarification.

"I've only been to see her once so far. What do you want the letter to say?"

Eliza seemed distracted, but she back-peddled a bit and said, "Oh, you can just have her write something about, 'Sarah has been seeing me for such-and-such number of sessions and we have discussed childhood issues.' Nothing fancy."

Apparently, I had previously misunderstood. Eliza didn't want a letter at the conclusion of therapy—she wanted one immediately. So, at my next session, I told the therapist what she needed to write. "The social worker asked me if you could send her the letter. Would you be able to do that?"

"Well," she responded with matter-of-fact yet delicate professionalism, "I'm not able to give a personal opinion about you or your progress. I can say that I've been seeing you, but I can't give any opinions."

"Oh, that's perfect." I assured her, "She only wants to know the dates you've seen me. She doesn't need an opinion."

Still, she told me, "I'm not comfortable writing a letter just yet. Let's talk about it after some more sessions." Why that statement didn't unfurl my mental red flag, I have no idea. I simply accepted her therapeutic expertise and went along with what she said.

After three or four more sessions, the therapist wrote the letter, sent it to West Coast, and we called it quits. She was a very nice lady, but as the therapy was no longer required for the home study, I was looking forward to using the exorbitant weekly fee on groceries rather than stirring up old dirt.

Walter and I spent the next several months prepping for our new addition to the Cavilry clan. We informed our bosses and coworkers of our adoption plan and the imminent possibility of a leave of absence with a new baby. I embarked upon cleaning and organizing the house in expectation of that longed-for little one. The most difficult task was gathering up all the required paperwork. I worked every spare moment to make and attend doctor appointments, fill out extensive forms, ask relatives for family histories, names, and birthdates, and harass people to write and send letters of recommendation for us. As Eliza wanted Heidi to be exposed to Down syndrome, I purchased tickets for The Pine Theater for Everyone, which produces plays performed by developmentally disabled young adults—an event which would have been fun for the family even if it hadn't been a mandatory assignment. I discovered and purchased movies about Down syndrome and mental retardation such as, *The Teachings of Jon*, and *Best Boy*. Heidi and I watched them together repeatedly, again, as we would have whether or not we were ordered to do so. We even named our new dog and cat Jon and Philly after the movies' starring characters. I also kept doing research on the Internet for available babies with Down syndrome.

The in-person interview with Eliza hadn't been a total disaster, but she had given me the understanding that she was very serious— this home study was being given great significance. As both Walter and I agreed, Eliza held our adoptive-parent-potentiality in her hands. We decided to do as she said and not bother her much with nagging phone calls. Her high-energy manner and I'm-so-busy demeanor had also made Walter and I wary about adding to her worry more than we had to.

But after several months of document-gathering went by without a word, I finally mentioned to Walter, "Would you mind calling Eliza and asking her what we need to do next?"

"Are you sure?" he worried. "I don't want to bug her and get her annoyed."

Since so much time had gone by, I insisted, "We really need to know what to do next. It's been months."

With hesitation, Walter called Eliza from his office phone. At the conclusion of the conversation, he called me back to give me the summary. "Apparently, she also expected *me* to go to therapy, and she wants me to go for several months."

I was livid. "Why didn't she tell us that at our interview? We could have started this months ago!"

Walter tried his best to calm me. "I know. There's nothing we can do about it now. I'm just going to start going. It's okay."

I didn't like Eliza. I wanted another social worker. Now I understood it was inept ability to communicate that had probably made the other couples at our adoption workshops crotchety. But I bit my tongue and trusted Walter. He started going to therapy that same week.

Once again, the weeks and months started passing by without a word from Eliza. After several more months, this time, I personally sucked up the courage to call her. I went ahead and dialed her cell phone number, and she answered.

"Hi, Eliza, it's Sarah Cavilry. I was just wondering what the next step was for us for our home study. You had mentioned wanting to interview our daughter?"

"Oh, yeah. I'm sorry I haven't called. I'm in the middle of a move—I have a lot going on right now. But I'll be driving through the Robinson Hills area, so I can meet you at your mom's house and interview Heidi."

I was thrilled to have another meeting—another step toward finding my baby and completing the home study. We made an appointment to meet at my mom's house the following week.

When the day for Heidi's interview came, we convened at Mom's with far fewer nerves. We were actually quite curious about what Heidi's interview would be like, and what she would say. My Little Mouse, at four years old, was a pretty little blonde girl with a truckload of personality. She was gregarious, curious, and full of fun and games. Always the performer, she loved to play Cinderella.

She requested and set up a game of Cinderella so often that Walter and I had her full preparatory instructional speech memorized. If we were driving in a car, she would beg us to play with her. When we submitted, she would coordinate the game: "Okay, I'm Cinderella. You're the good stepmother [in her game, good and not evil]. In the right chair [the passenger seat] is Anastasia and Drizella and I make them talk. Okay? Okay. Now, where were we? Oh, yes, I remember."

She would then begin speaking to us as Cinderella or a step sister and we had to respond as the good stepmother. This would go on for hours if we were patient enough and had the mental stamina to keep up the improvisation for that long.

Cinderella usually won out, but pretending to be a multitude of different characters was, by far, her greatest joy: a new girl at school, a character from a movie, a talking animal. She was very creative and her pretend play was almost always an avenue for her to discuss and act out what she had heard or learned or saw and wanted to work through.

Although Heidi's outspoken honesty in an interview might be a potential embarrassment, we were confident that it would be the kind of parental humiliation that would be looked back on with fondness and related to friends and relatives for years.

Walter and I, daughter in tow, sat down with Mom at her front-room breakfast table so we could watch out the window for Eliza's arrival. Knowing I was, as usual, nervous, Mom did her best to keep conversation bubbly and light, as is, for her, also usual.

I always find a relaxing familiarity in Mom's presence. She's an almost-exact physical copy of me, save the shortness of her red hair and the immense length of mine—and a difference in age of 30 years. She's good-natured, eager to please, and very attentive to the needs and wants of others—she taught me the joy of giving and the relishing of pleasure given to all people.

I wasn't surprised to see mom jump up immediately to attend to our guest's needs when Eliza arrived and, without a hello, immediately demanded, "I need you to feed me. I drove a long way and I'm starving."

The little devil on my shoulder told me it was presumptuous and rude that Eliza came in demanding that my 68-year-old mother provide breakfast; however, the angel on the opposite side told me that Eliza held the key to our rejection or acceptance as an adoptive family, and we should appease her hunger in order to keep her as agreeable as possible.

While sitting with the four of us, eating her cereal, granola bar, banana, and drinking her coffee (made to order), Eliza complained.

"I'm having so much trouble with my daughter right now. I sent her to science camp, and she says she hates it. She called me begging to come home. But I need somewhere for her to go while I move to my new place. In fact, your mom's house is on the way to my new house. After this interview, I'm going straight to Redding. I have so much on my mind right now, and so much to do—I really don't want my daughter to come home right now. There would be nothing for her to do, and nothing for her to help with. She'd just get in the way."

Apparently, Eliza would be taking a position as the director of an adoption agency up in northern California. Her busy and distracted mind racing, she went from one topic to the next like a tornado jumping from house to house. She landed on the topic of colleagues at work.

"I drive my coworkers crazy. I always say, 'Who's your boss?' and they say back, 'Jesus is.' They say it all annoyed, and they laugh at me. They call me a cheerleader for Jesus. I make them nuts!"

"Oh, ha ha ha," we forced out through our awkward secular smiles.

By this time, my weirdness alarm was going off full-blast. Sign language interpreters have a very strict code of ethics, as do, I believe, social workers. Eliza's lack of professional distance was causing me great discomfort. But Eliza held the power of approval. Smile and nod; just smile and nod.

Having consumed her breakfast and spilled her guts, Eliza finally began the interview.

"So, Heidi, I am going to ask you some questions, okay?"

In true Heidi style, she replied, "Look what I can do." She then proceeded to put both cupped hands over her mouth and breathe loudly, deeply, and slowly. Then she quoted in kind, "The Force is with you, young Skywalker. But you are not a Jedi yet."

Thoroughly entertained, Walter, Mom and I chuckled heartily, logging that moment into our mental hard-drives for future sharing.

Eliza was far less amused. "That was very interesting," she told Heidi, "but I need you to concentrate on answering my questions, okay? Let's get on with the interview."

Our grins faded slowly and our giggles tapered off—we folded our hands in our laps and got on with the interview.

"So," Eliza continued, "how do you feel about the possibility of having a baby brother or sister?"

"Good." Heidi was making the salt and pepper shakers talk to each other.

"Now, I need you to listen closely and pay attention." I took Mrs. Salt and Mrs. Pepper away and whispered to Heidi to pay attention.

Eliza went on. "Do you understand that your baby brother or sister will have something called Down syndrome?"

"Yeah."

"I need you to understand that your brother or sister will always be slower than you."

"Uh huh."

"They will never learn as much as you."

"Yep."

"Do you understand?"

I didn't like this line of questioning at all. To Heidi, a four-year-old, the baby was going to be just that and nothing more—a baby. The little newborn wasn't going to be some retarded, Jell-O-y blob that was different from all of the images and expectations Heidi had previously formulated. My daughter had no expectations at all—she just wanted a baby. Why did Eliza feel the need to teach Heidi that the baby would be "different"? Why did Eliza believe the baby was something that a four-year-old needed to be emotionally prepared for?

My beautiful daughter answered, "Yeah, I understand. I'm going to teach the baby to eat with a spoon and change his diaper and I'll give him a bottle and sing him to sleep. And I'm going to make a steering wheel for his car seat so it will rock back and forth when he steers it."

"But you understand that the baby won't be able to learn as much as you."

Dang, Eliza was determined.

"Yeah." Heidi simply didn't care about that. She just didn't care. And I felt deeply that it didn't matter. The fact that the baby would know less only seemed to gladden Heidi with the possibility of becoming a mentor for a tiny sibling. Purposely forming a prejudice in my young daughter's impressionable mind went against everything I believed proper and right. But I kept my mouth shut and kept in mind that Heidi would probably never remember this meeting anyway, and soon there would be an end to this home study and I'd be holding my daughter's sibling in my arms.

"Okay," Eliza concluded, gathering up her paperwork, "I'm done. I'm going to be busy with the move, but I'll have the home study written up in August." It was July, but I was glad to have an approximate time frame to let me see that the end was a mere month away. Eliza left, taking a granola bar for the road.

As soon as Eliza's car pulled away from the front curb, my mom took a pause from bubbly acceptance to note, "I don't think I liked her much." She mirrored my sentiments precisely.

Chapter 9:

Time

Not wanting our home study to become an additional point of stress in her already stressed-out personal life, I didn't contact Eliza when August came and went, spending my time instead working 40 hours a week, studying for my bachelor's degree, and raising my daughter. But in December, Robin called us from Cincinnati to ask us if we were interested in an unborn Californian girl with Down syndrome. We were thrilled by the possibility of a baby girl Cavilry. I decided this was the time to give Eliza a gentle nudge.

I emailed her: "We were wondering what the next steps are for us to take to complete the home study process. We just found out about an unborn baby with Down syndrome in California, and we'd like to be available to adopt her. Let us know as soon as you're able what we need to do."

Eliza's response was immediate and shocking. The telling sentence in her email read, "There were action steps that Walter was supposed to take that to my knowledge have never been done."

I was dumbfounded. Eliza hadn't contacted us in months. How could she come to any conclusions, positive or negative, about what steps had been completed or neglected? I wrote back right away.

"We did everything you told us to do immediately after we met with you. I'm sorry if I did anything to lead you to believe that we weren't enthusiastic about completing the home study."

She did not respond. Three days later, we got a call from Shawna Cikos, the director of West Coast. Shawna asked us to come in as soon as we could to discuss the home study. I was relieved that someone else was taking over the home study process, as Eliza seemed to have, actively and decisively, dropped the ball. We made an appointment to meet with Shawna at her office.

I gathered up the last bit of required paraphernalia which remained uncollected from Eliza's original list: two copies of our marriage certificate and 10 family photos to distribute to various birth parents looking to find adoptive families. I wanted to deliver these to West Coast in person since postage to send a heavy envelope of photos was an avoidable expense. I put them all in a manila envelope which I held proudly in my lap as Walter and I drove to West Coast during this work-approved extended lunch hour. We traveled the 10 Freeway with a jointly peaceful feeling for a new beginning with a new social worker, and for the nearing completion of what had been difficult months of preparation. We had wanted to adopt a baby while Heidi was three, but the long adoption process and Eliza's procrastination had lasted a year and a half, bringing our daughter to nearly 5 years old.

Heidi would soon start kindergarten, and we wanted to raise her in the best possible schools. Walter and I moved back to my hometown of Robinson Hills so that she could attend Cherry Elementary, my alma mater. We found our dream home—a yellow and white four-bedroom bungalow on a quiet corner lot with a big back yard, a koi pond, and two—count 'em—*two* fireplaces. The best part: Cherry Elementary was right around the corner. We knew this house was a keeper for life.

With a new home in a quiet suburb, we felt even more ready for an addition to the family, and an actual unborn baby waiting for us added to our excitement. Walking up the steps to the West Coast office, imagining still more new beginnings, we giggled and teased each other like giddy newlyweds; while Walter teased, I playfully whacked him with the manila envelope I was holding.

Soon after our arrival, Shawna came out of her office and met us in the lobby. She was very tall—over six feet—proportionally thin with long, waist-length, jet-black hair and a youthful face—at least a decade and a half younger than me. She greeted us with professional warmth.

"Walter and Sarah?"

Walter shook her hand and responded, "Yes, and you must be Shawna. We've heard so much about you," as was his standard greeting for people he's never heard anything about before. With a smile and a courteous chuckle, Shawna directed us into the conference room.

Shawna sat at the head of the long table with Walter and me in two comfy office-chairs at her left-hand side. My husband, as is his usual conduct, created a relaxed atmosphere with some of his traditional humorous banter. At least he tried to—until Shawna got down to the real business at hand.

"I'm afraid I have to say something that you're not going to like."

I felt the blood drain from my face. Shawna continued.

"I have several concerns, and I'm afraid I'm not going to be able to approve your home study at this time."

I was in complete shock, at an absolute loss to understand what she could consider unapprovable. Weren't we just a typical family? Weren't we simply another couple wanting to adopt? Walter verbalized what was running through my confused brain.

"What's wrong? What specifically?"

"I just have some concerns about your marriage."

I remembered telling Eliza that we'd had problems after three years of marriage. But I told her we'd been to therapy and we were much better now—better than ever. And Eliza had verbally assured us that our past difficulties were normal and acceptable. Shawna continued.

"Before I can approve your home study, you're going to need to go to marriage counseling."

Seriously? More counseling? Naturally, I would comply with whatever we were instructed to do, but there was an unborn baby waiting for us. What if we couldn't get the home study completed in time to be an eligible match for that waiting girl?

"Of course we'll do that. But how long do you want us to go to therapy before you can approve us?"

"I can't say for certain, but it will probably need to be at least three months."

I wasn't aware that I had still more blood in my head to drain out, but apparently I did. That available little girl, if we had to follow through with Shawna's requirements, would definitely not be ours. Feeling goals and dreams slip away, I began to panic.

We told Eliza that Walter and I had worked—*seriously*—on our marriage with months of professional therapy already. Why was that no good? Why did we have to go through that again? And now? I told Shawna so. She replied,

"You need to have a very strong marriage to adopt."

Walter reiterated my previous question, "But what is it specifically that you're concerned about?"

"I just have some concerns about your marriage."

It became obvious that she wasn't going to tell us. A feeling of hopelessness began to overwhelm me. I started crying. I felt judged and, most of all, misunderstood. "I wish there was some way for you to see us while we're at home. We're happy. We have a good family."

"But there are certain concerns—very big concerns—that I have about your marriage. Frankly, the idea of putting a child into your home scares me."

She had concerns about us as a couple that were so grave as to terrify her about the thought of a child in our presence. Shawna had never met us before. What was she talking about? What in the world could Eliza have told her?

I let her know, "But you don't even know us!"

Shawna responded with a definitive, "Well, I'm sorry about that. But it's my decision."

She didn't have the first idea who the Cavilrys were, and she had made a devastatingly concrete decision about us. But there was more.

"I'm also concerned about the letter from your therapist." The letter which only said I'd gone to sessions on such-and-such dates? That letter was a concern?

I asked, "What concerned you about that?"

"Well, I can't disclose what was said in her personal letter to me, but you did not go nearly enough. Eliza wanted you to attend therapy for at least a year."

I was flabbergasted. "A year? She never said that. She wanted a letter right away."

Shawna didn't seem concerned by any possible lacking communication. She went on.

"Also, you want to adopt a child with a disability, right?"

Walter answered for both of us. "Right."

"Well, raising a child with disabilities is *hard*!" She said this as if she was giving us vital and awful information, echoing the big deal Eliza had made out of Down syndrome.

What did Eliza and Shawna think Down syndrome meant? Did they think the baby would be a monster? An alien? A Warner Brothers Tasmanian devil in need of restraint and a gag before it destroyed our house and ate our pets?

I defended myself. "I've worked with people with Down syndrome since I was 16, and I've researched Down syndrome extensively. I'm not going into this blindly!"

"Well anyway, I've made my decision, and now we need to move on."

"But there is a baby waiting. We did everything we were told to do. When we last saw Eliza, she told us she'd write our home study in August, and now it's January. If she had told us what to do, we would have done anything. This is completely unfair."

"Well, I'm sorry you feel that way, but that is my decision and now we need to move on from here. If you're not happy with my decision, you're more than welcome to look for another agency. So, was there anything else?"

I was sitting there like an idiot, holding copies of my marriage certificate and 10 pictures of our family. I felt like a moron.

"Eliza said we also needed to have these for our home study." I slid them to her and she didn't touch them. She looked at them like they were useless.

Still crying, I stood. As I turned and started out of the conference room door, Shawna actually patted me on the back. I wanted to reach out and snatch her hand clean off of her wrist. How could she dare to try and comfort me? I would have preferred she spend two seconds trying to understand us and our situation rather than wasting that moment on a perfunctory back-pat.

We walked out of the West Coast office, Walter with his arm around me, my head on his shoulder, tears rushing down my cheeks in rivers like a grieving anime character. When we got into the car and Walter put the keys in the ignition, I blurted out,

"Let's go to Disneyland."

With the world looking, to me, like a devastatingly gray winter hailstorm, I needed a little rainbow in the form of the happiest place on earth. I called work to say my meeting hadn't gone well and I wouldn't be back that day. My coworkers consoled me, told me West Coast could take a long walk, and wished me a relaxing day with the big mouse.

Walter and I, before heading for Anaheim, made a detour to Heidi's child care. When we parked in front of the bright kelly-green house and I went into the play yard gate to retrieve my child, I saw Kendra, the director of Caring Days Daycare. So many times, I had fantasized about our new baby going to Caring Days. Kendra had been watching our daughter every work day since Heidi was three months old, and we trusted that our second child would be safe and happy there, big sister teaching her the ropes. When I saw Kendra's bright, smiling face, smooth, dark skin, and soft motherly form, and heard her usual, peppy, "Hi Sarah! How was *your* day," I couldn't prevent bursting into a new wave of tears.

"The adoption agency rejected us."

Kendra looked at me, stunned. "What? They rejected you? Why? You're wonderful parents. And there are so many disabled children that need homes." She wrapped her arms around me. "It's just not right. Please let me know if there's anything I can do. I'll help you in any way I can." I saw that she was crying as well.

I was endlessly grateful for the words from Kendra and my coworkers to help me believe I wasn't the world's worst mother, wife, and human. I now understood the reason why the home study process was considered so emotionally difficult. Save the death of my twins, having my dreams torn away via this personal, unjustified rejection was the worst emotional trauma I had ever experienced.

As we began our drive down the 10 Freeway, I tried to explain to Heidi why Mommy was crying. Using my best five-year-old vocabulary, I explained.

"You know how we were trying to adopt a baby?"

"Yeah. The baby died?"

"No, we don't have a baby yet. There are some people who have to say if we can have a baby or not."

"Uh huh. They said we can't have a baby?"

"Yeah. That's what they said. We're not giving up, but Mommy is really upset right now."

"Why did they say we can't have a baby?"

I answered honestly. "I don't know, Honey. They think we wouldn't be good parents."

"What?" Heidi shouted, incensed. "You're the best parents ever." I wasn't surprised she said that—she often compliments us on being awesome. But I was particularly grateful for her words of validation and trust at that moment.

She continued. "That's so mean. If I saw those people, I would go right up and say, 'You know what I have for you? Here it is.' And I would punch them right in the face."

Tears dripped over my involuntary smile. "I know, baby. I wish you could do that."

When we arrived, I did my best to let the magic of the Magic Kingdom do its work. That was a difficult task—the weight of depression on my chest was heavy and omnipresent. I knew that, tomorrow, I would begin the task of trying to convince West Coast they were wrong. While sitting in front of Sleeping Beauty's Castle, Walter called his therapist and made an appointment for us for the following day. We would begin couples therapy as Shawna instructed, but waiting for three months before recommencing the home study process would mean giving up the chance of adopting the available, developing baby girl. We had the option of going to another agency and trying all over again for a successful home study, but we had spent months—almost two years—trying to complete this process, and $2,000 of our money was in West Coast's bank account. I couldn't just walk away without giving it one last try.

Walter had the same idea. While I waited with Heidi for popcorn, he gave Shawna one last call. We both wanted to make sure we were working on the precise issues that Shawna—and apparently, Eliza— had concerns about. So Walter asked Shawna on the phone for clarification: What exactly was it about our marriage that needed work, and why was the idea of a child in our home scary? Walter couldn't get any clear response to either issue, as Shawna only restated and re-restated that there were concerns about our marriage. Oh, and that "scary" was the wrong word choice, and she apologized for having picked that particular word. On that day, questions were going to remain unanswered.

Standing in line for the Peter Pan ride, thinking about life, unfairness, and unrealized dreams, a new tear made its way down my cheek. My daughter, the greatest love and purest joy of my existence, looked up at me with her big blue eyes and said, "You're crying *again*?" I couldn't help but laugh.

Every single day from Heidi's birth until that point, I had been grateful for the presence of my angel, my Little Mouse, but never more than that exact moment. Even if I never adopted a child, my life would still be complete.

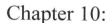

Chapter 10:

Pleas

The next day, I went to my office with swollen, red eyes, but with my chin up and shoulders back, ready to get to work. If we quietly went along with Shawna's requirements for months of therapy, this adoption opportunity would be completely lost. In between office tasks, just in case issues with West Coast couldn't be resolved, I did some searches for adoption agencies in the southern California area. On a referral website, I filled out my contact information to be notified of different agencies which matched our location and needs. But rather than solely automated assistance, I also reached out for real, live help.

I started out with a call to my ex-therapist. I wanted to find out what was in her letter that Shawna couldn't disclose.

After the perfunctory courteous greeting when she answered, I asked her what she had written. Her response was brief and professional.

"I said the dates of your sessions and for how many minutes you were here for each one."

Benign.

Then she added, "Something that might be a question to them was—I did say I felt you could benefit from additional therapy."

Malignant.

What happened to not being allowed to give an opinion? I hung up soon after. There wasn't much else to say.

I'm not sure why I never pursued any retribution for the part she took in the failure of the home study, especially when I later found out that the therapists' agency originally referred by Eliza and which I attended was a unit established and run by West Coast—the very definition of *conflict of interest*.

I couldn't bring myself to give up, but I didn't know what I possibly could do, or who I could go to for help. I floundered and grasped as I racked my brain for any idea that would benefit our ability to see the home study to completion. Who was out there that could help us?

Then I remembered Phyllis, the first person at West Coast I was initially referred to. She had been so nice and personable, and seemed to have experience with adopting disabled children. I thought I'd contact her with a plea, begging her for support. I sent her an email.

> Dear Phyllis,
>
> I met with Shawna yesterday. She said she cannot approve our home study until Walter and I go to couples counseling for three months. But there is a baby available now, and this delay is going to cause us to lose the opportunity to adopt this baby.
>
> I'm reaching out to see if there is anything at all you can do to help us. We are desperate for assistance from someone.
>
> I'm so sorry for bothering you, but I don't know where else to turn.
>
> Sincerely,
> Sarah

Simultaneously, unbeknownst to me, Walter was calling Phyllis by phone to have the exact conversation I was initiating with her via email. The moment I clicked *send* was probably the same moment Walter was hearing the words, "I'm uncomfortable being put in the middle."

Less than 15 minutes later, my office phone rang. It was Walter.

"Shawna is on the other line and she wants to have a word with us."

He switched to conference call mode and announced, "I have Sarah on the line now, Shawna. You had something you wanted to say?" Walter's voice was overtly matter-of-fact rather than customarily charming, making me wonder what they had already discussed before bringing me into the conversation.

Shawna began, "Hello, Sarah."

"Hi," I responded, adding a traditional, "How are you?"

She unexpectedly responded with the nonstandard, "Not very good, I'll be honest with you." Her voice didn't sound depressed or blue, like she'd been having a bad day. Shawna sounded like she was doing all she could to hold back an angry tirade. "You emailed Phyllis when I told you already what my decision was. Phyllis is not the director of West Coast. I am the director of West Coast."

Shawna's voice was fast, loud, and full of energy. She sounded livid.

"Also, I saw that you've been looking for a new adoption agency."

How did she know? Oh, I had filled out a referral form online, and my application must have been forwarded to agencies to enable them to contact new clients directly. I instantly felt a bit stupid, naïve of 21st century technology. Still, Shawna's reaction to my referral-seeking confused me.

"That shows a complete lack of trust. Therefore, I am closing your home study and we will no longer be working with you. So, good luck in your life."

I had felt so low the previous day. As the result of this particular phone call, my hopes dove 100 times lower. I reached out for help—pleaded for help—and Phyllis, within a mere 15 minutes, had turned on me. She told on me. Absolutely no one was on our side. I felt emotionally all alone and so completely misunderstood.

I tried to explain myself by beginning, "I never meant to offend you—"

But she cut me off with a loud, sing-songy reply, "Oh, *I'm* not *offen*ded." She went on outlining the details of our rejection, but I could no longer understand her words. My body and mind went numb. I couldn't believe what was occurring.

In true Walter form, he stepped up for a logical debate, even with this irrational woman.

"Now, let me ask you a question. If looking for a new agency means you can no longer trust us, then why did you tell us when we had our meeting that we can look for a new agency?"

With the same mockingly tuneful tone, Shawna replied, "Oh, *I* don't *care* if you *find* a new *agen*cy." I felt like I was on the elementary-school playground and she was the class bully. Her voice told us she couldn't wait for us to leave—good-bye and good riddance.

She reiterated, "And, as I said, I've made my decision. So, good luck, and..."

Walter interrupted her second attempt at good-bye with a challenge. "You were ready to let us go, back when we first met, weren't you?"

Without pause, Shawna blurted her admission firmly: "Yes, I was."

I couldn't believe this was happening. Never having met us, receiving second-hand and inaccurate information from Eliza, not knowing us at all, she thought us such undesirable humans as to be completely inappropriate for the task of raising children. I questioned my own ability to raise Heidi. I thought about the family pictures we had taken—laughing, playing, a happy family, ready to take in a new addition. I felt like a sham.

I heard Walter say, "I have one more question."

Shawna's rapid response echoed in my barely-functioning brain, "I'm not interested in any more questions."

Walter convinced her to listen, but my mind completely shut down. Quietly, hearing Shawna and Walter's dispute fade away, I gently set the phone handset down on the receiver.

I sat at my desk, staring down at the dusty faux-oak tabletop. I was frozen by the shock of what had just happened.

Soon, I felt delicate arms reach around my shoulders and a soft cheek press against mine.

"I'm sorry." It was my coworker and friend, Anna. At about 80 pounds and less than five feet tall, my beautiful Indonesian buddy could have blown away in a mild breeze. However, at that moment, there was nothing bigger, more enveloping, or more appreciated than her consoling embrace.

Once again, I began to cry. But I felt certain—how could I be a terrible person? No one that rotten could have such great friends. Through my sadness and disappointment, I knew I could still be thankful for my amazing life and the beautiful people in it.

While I sat quietly at my desk, from his own office, Walter called Shawna's supervisor, Violet, to discuss what had just happened. Later on, he gave me the summary of their conversation. Apparently, Violet had asked Walter, "What do you want *me* to do about it?" I wasn't sure if she had asked Walter that particular question out of true interest in helping, or as a way of being snide. That answer would come later.

I felt such an emotional loneliness. That feeling of hopelessness was compounded exponentially by the time constraints involved. I mechanically performed my work duties, but the failing home study process never left my thoughts. Throughout most of the workday, I was running from class to class interpreting for deaf students. Walter, however, spent the day in one office and was easily reachable by phone. He had the misfortune of getting desperate calls from me all day long asking pointless should-you, can-we, will-you-please questions. But really, it all came down to the fact that time was running out and we needed someone to be on our side. I thought fleetingly and illogically of my parents, but knew, of course, there was nothing they could do. I imagined giving up, and the thought broke my heart—all the dreams and all the work for nothing. My mind went back to finding someone to help us. I was tired and confused and feeling so desperate for someone to take us under their wing and be on our side. Who could help? Who would understand?

Oprah. Oprah Winfrey could help us. She was making dreams come true every day for people who needed luxury cars and the world's best fuzzy socks. The logical, still-working part of my brain knew her assistants' assistants would read the first three words of my emailed plea and delete it. The desperate, no-longer-functioning part of my brain thought there was a chance Oprah could help and, since I had no one else to turn to, I should go ahead and beg for her to make it all better.

The desperate part of my brain won. I found Oprah's website and an email address, and I wrote a letter to my cyber savior, summarizing my plight and plea and clicked *send*. I have no memory of what I wrote. What could I possibly have said? "Dear Oprah, West Coast is being mean and they hurt my feelings. Could you please make it all better?" I felt silly. The chance of her helping me was the longest of long shots, but if I didn't try, there was a 0% chance of getting her help. An attempt meant to me, at least, a possibility.

* * *

At home the following weekend, I stood in our back yard looking over the fence into our koi pond. The previous owner of our house, a single mother, had built that entire pond, landscaped surrounding banks, fountained filters, and all with her own hands. My father had just made his weekly call to see how I was fairing with adulthood and I was letting him know. Shawna might not have been willing to tell us the exact reasons for rejecting our case, but, after filling out the necessary consent forms for disclosure, Shawna freely told Walter's therapist. Wishing for the comfort of childhood, I gave Pops the summary of our woes.

"The director of the adoption agency thinks Walter and I have an at-risk marriage, even though we've been to months of therapy and have felt happy together for years. And she said Walter and I have too *rosy* an outlook on disabilities. But there are disabled children out there with no families. Does she think no one should adopt them?"

My father, a man with a big heart and a loss for words during hard times, simply stated, "Well, maybe it wasn't meant to be."

It wasn't meant to be. A dream I've had since I was a teen and held onto as an adult just, succinctly, wasn't meant to be? Who gets to decide that? Dad? I understood what my dad meant and what the intentions were for making that comment; he had probably only said that to console me. However, his statement did the best thing for my deflated self-confidence that any one sentence could have done. It prompted the defiant adolescent in me to resurface.

I wanted to prove him wrong.

Reality hit me. I had felt so alone and helpless, nobody on my side, so completely by myself that I tried getting help from Oprah. Jeez.

But there *was* someone to help. Me. *Myself.* Dammit, I was the one with the dreams and goals. Fulfilling my desires wasn't anyone's responsibility but my own. I was worthy of the adoption experience, and I was the one who had to make it happen. I could make it happen.

In that moment, talking to Dad whisked me out of my self-pitying lethargy. Maybe he was my protector when I was a kid, and maybe Oprah was savior for people with cold piggies, but I was a big, grown-up girl now. People adopted children every day, and I could do the same.

Thanks to Dad, from that moment on, totally absent of malice but full of ambition, I couldn't wait for the day when I could say, "See? It *was* meant to be." I was unconsciously indebted to my father for snapping me out of my depression and back into constructive action.

Chapter 11:

Answers

My first task was to get some of that $2,000 home-study fee back. I began the process by taking several days to compose a detailed letter to West Coast explaining the reasons why we had complaints with their agency and why we deserved a return of our payment. During this period of perfecting prose, I received an official memo from Shawna in our home mailbox.

In her letter, Shawna stated the reason for closing our home study: 1) our lack of involvement in the process, indicated by our inability to complete assignments given to us by our case worker, and 2) my email to Phyllis after having been told not to contact her. There was no mention of our search for a new agency, our alleged marital issues, or our positive outlook regarding disabled children. I was amazed by the varied contradictions, composed in an official paper correspondence from the adoption agency she directed. There was no way I was going to allow this slapdash organization to keep our $2,000.

With Shawna's note as added fuel, I completed my letter.

Eliza Richmond, Social Worker
West Coast Child and Family Services
11342 Carnation Dr.
Marina del Rey, CA 90292

Dear Ms. Richmond,

I am now following through with West Coast Child and Family Services' Grievance Procedure, Step I: "Should you have any questions, concerns or complaints, first discuss these with your West Coast social worker."

As we have, today, received a letter stating that West Coast has decided not to continue with our adoption home study, we are now not certain whether you can still be considered our social worker. However, we want to follow proper procedures, so we will address this letter to you. In case we were in error in our interpretation of Step I, we will CC this letter to Shawna Cikos, Adoption Coordinator, and Violet Coolidge, Program Director.

We have several concerns and complaints.

Your instructions to us regarding procedures we needed to follow in order to complete our home study were severely lacking in clarity. Here are several examples:

1) When you visited Sarah at her house for her personal interview, you stated that you would not approve the home study unless she went to therapy to deal with childhood issues. Sarah, within a day, began making the necessary phone calls to begin the therapy process.

You then, after less than two weeks, told Sarah that you were wondering where the letter was from her therapist, as you had not yet received it. Sarah was confused by this, because she thought that people generally went to therapy for more than a session or two in order to deal with any issue; however, as a layman who trusted her social worker's expertise, she agreed to tell her therapist that you wanted the letter immediately. Sarah's therapist wrote the letter after several more sessions, when the therapist said she was comfortable writing the letter.

It was very recently that Sarah called her therapist again and found out that you had stated that you expected Sarah should go to therapy for an entire year. By telling Sarah to immediately get a letter, there was no indication of any kind that she should have gone to therapy for a year, and that time frame was certainly never stated. As the social worker and the person who was in charge of our case, it was of the utmost importance that your expectations for us be laid out as clearly as possible.

Nevertheless, Sarah made every possible effort to do what she was told to do, showing her enthusiasm and willingness to participate effectively in the home study process.

2) When you visited Walter at his house for his personal interview, you said absolutely nothing which resembled, "You must go to therapy." Walter did not receive any indication, hint, or inkling from you that he was required to attend therapy in order to have our home study approved. Therefore, he was, obviously, unaware that he must go to therapy. Therefore, he did not go.

After several months, when Walter called you to find out what we were supposed to be doing next, you told him for the first time that he was required to go to therapy. This added several months onto the home study process. Once again, your inability to properly convey what was necessary for us to do cost us greatly.

In response, Walter immediately called his therapist to begin weekly sessions with her, and he has been seeing her ever since (he is presently still working with her.)

Clearly, Walter, like Sarah, made every possible effort to do what he was told to do, showing his enthusiasm and willingness to participate effectively in the home study process.

3) When you interviewed our daughter, Heidi, in Sarah's mother's house, one of the last things you told us before you began your drive to Redding was, "I will write up your home study in August."

As a result of this statement, we were of the belief that the home study process was going smoothly with you. The fact that it was not going smoothly was a complete shock to us.

It would have been completely appropriate and appreciated if, at Sarah's mother's house, you had said something more honest, like, "After you and Walter have both gone to therapy for [at least X amount of] months, I will write up your home study."

If you thought you might write up our home study in August but you later changed your mind, you should have communicated your decision with us the moment you changed your mind. If you were simply placating us and had no intention of writing our home study in August, then we don't need to express to you how that inhibits proper communication.

4) When Sarah contacted you once again after several months to see what else we needed to do to complete our home study, you stated to Sarah via email sent January 5, that "there were action steps that Walter was supposed to take that to my knowledge have never been done."

There was absolutely no reason for you to assume that Walter had never done what you told him to. We have always done exactly everything that you told us to do, and to assume such things about either one of us misrepresents our personalities and our commitment to the home study process.

If you had any reason to believe that Walter had not completed something you wanted him to do, it would have been appropriate for you to communicate with either one of us and ask whether or not we were taking the steps you had directed us to take, rather than assume we hadn't.

Above all, you should definitely never have stated blind assumptions to your coworkers or supervisors as if they were facts. That was dishonest and damaging, not only to our case but to the life of a child who is in need of a home.

Regarding your behavior at our final meeting at Sarah's mother's house, we have some general complaints that relate to your lack of professionalism and dedication to the seriousness of our home study.

1) As we were very serious about wishing to concentrate on the issue of Heidi's interview, it was highly inappropriate of you to spend the majority of the meeting talking about the family problems you were having with your daughter, her messages to you begging to be allowed to come home from summer camp, and your inability to properly care for her while you participated in your move from Los Angeles to Redding. That was none of our business, and it was uncomfortable conversation for that particular meeting, especially in front of our daughter and Sarah's mother.

2) In our meetings with you, you asked us about religion, and we told you that we were not religious people. However, at Sarah's mother's house, you preached to us about God/Jesus Christ. This was highly inappropriate and uncomfortable, as we have seen nothing in the literature for West Coast Child and Family Services associating it with a Christian organization.

We sincerely hope that our lack of religion was not the cause of a conscious decision on your part to misrepresent us to Shawna Cikos or anyone else at West Coast Child and Family Services.

Since we began communicating with Shawna Cikos on January 22, there have been several incidences that we take grievance with, and we will list them here, in compliance with Step I of the West Coast Child and Family Services' Grievance Procedure.

1) When Ms. Cikos met with us for the first time, it was after no one at all from West Coast Child and Family Services had contacted or spoken to us for seven months.

In preface, we have always worked on our relationship, since we feel that every marriage requires adaptation and development in order to maintain a healthy growth. After your interviews with us at our home, we took the opportunity to address issues that we felt had come to .light, as our goal is to do whatever possible to create a loving and joyous household for ourselves and our daughter.

However, without ever having met us, and without pursuing an update on our therapy or the current status of our relationship, Ms. Cikos made grave assumptions about our marriage, and our ability to parent, stating:

a) "The thought of putting a child in your home scares me."

b) "You need to take time to heal your relationship."

Regarding a), to this day, we don't understand what it was about us which scared Ms. Cikos, especially since she had never previously met us, spoken to us, or consulted our therapists. Ms. Cikos has since told us that "scared" was the wrong word and that she apologizes; however, Ms. Cikos has yet to tell us the *right* word, continuing to leave us perplexed as to what it is about us which frightened her so.

Regarding b), neither Ms. Cikos nor anyone at West Coast Child and Family Services had talked to us in many, many months. Although we had spent well over a year working on our relationship until it had reached its present state of stability and happiness, as we told Ms. Cikos in order to update her, Ms. Cikos still insisted that we needed to *begin* to heal. Attempts we made to explain our progress were entirely ignored by Ms. Cikos, and she stated several times that, no matter what had occurred in the past months, she would not change her decision that we needed serious help. Rather than productively converse with us and address the issues we were bringing up, she simply ignored our statements and said, "If you do not think West Coast is giving you what you need, you can go elsewhere." She then went on to repeat this sentiment several times during the remainder of our meeting.

During the time of this meeting with Ms. Cikos, not only was communication ineffective, but it was entirely nonexistent, as she seemed to not even be able to hear what we were saying to her.

After the meeting, we told each other that we strongly felt that Ms. Shawna Cikos didn't care what we said or what evidence we gave her to prove that we have a strong, stable marriage; Ms. Cikos seemed determined to reject the possibility of bringing a child into our home, even if we were completely qualified and approvable.

2) During our meeting with Ms. Shawna Cikos on January 22, she stated several times that raising a child with a disability is very difficult. She later stated to Walter's therapist that one of the reasons she was uncomfortable approving our case was because of Sarah's belief that adopting a child with Down syndrome was going to be "all rosy" (those were the therapist's words which she used to summarize what Ms. Cikos had said.)

During the January 22 meeting, it was explained to Ms. Cikos that Sarah had had over 20 years of experience working with the developmentally disabled, and that her positive life experiences with Down syndrome were her reasons for wanting to bring this kind of child into the family. The Cavilry family has, over the past several years, made attempts to introduce all members of the household to individuals with Down syndrome, causing Walter to become influenced by the love and caring that this population generally possesses, resulting in Walter's desire and eagerness to raise a child with Down syndrome.

Parents who give birth to or adopt an able-bodied child are excited about the prospect of raising and loving a child; a child with Down syndrome deserves to have the same excitement revolve around their coming into the world. Someone like Sarah who has extended experience with this population is just the person to give that excited welcome to a deserving child who happens to have Down syndrome. Someone like Walter, who is a devoted, attentive and concerned father, is just the right person to raise a disabled child with love and happiness.

To say that the Cavilry family's willingness to take a disabled child into their home is one of the reasons for reluctance to complete the home study seems to be a complete negation of what a social services agency should be in support of.

There happens to be a list of over 200 families in the United States waiting to adopt children with Down syndrome. If Ms. Cikos disagrees with those parents, then maybe she should try to find out what it is that all of those families know that she doesn't, rather than using her prejudice against the disabled to inhibit disabled children's abilities to enter into loving households.

3) Walter called Phyllis Greenberg on January 23, and this was the time when Ms. Greenberg told Walter she was uncomfortable being put in the middle. Sarah, however, was not present for the conversation. As a result, Sarah contacted Ms. Greenberg without the knowledge that Walter had been told that Ms. Greenberg was uncomfortable being contacted.

If contacting Ms. Greenberg was such a grave offence as to anger Ms. Cikos beyond the ability to communicate appropriately (please see below), then this information should have been given to both marriage partners in writing. If the time necessary to formally notify both husband and wife was not available, then the fact that Walter spoke to Phyllis on the phone and Sarah contacted

Phyllis separately should have been taken into calm consideration.

4) As stated previously, Ms. Cikos noted to us several times during our face-to-face meeting that, if we were unhappy, we could go elsewhere to complete a home study. This sentiment caused us to feel that we ought to look elsewhere, in case we were unable to complete our home study with West Coast Child and Family Services. Sarah filled out two internet-based referral forms to try to find a new agency with which to complete an adoption home study.

This leads us to the description of the unfortunate phone conversation that took place with Ms. Shawna Cikos on January 23.

Ms. Cikos called Walter at work; Walter called Sarah at her desk so the three participants could have a conference call.

When Sarah said to Ms. Cikos, "How are you," Ms. Cikos replied, "Not very good, I'll be honest with you."

Ms. Cikos then went on to say that our email to Ms. Greenberg and our attempts at finding other agencies to perform a home study proved to her that we were untrustworthy, and "West Coast" no longer wanted to handle our home study case.

Sarah and Walter both noticed that Ms. Cikos's voice was extremely agitated and the sound level was very high, indicating to both of us that Ms. Cikos was particularly angry, supported by her initial indication to us that she was "not very good."

Walter and Sarah both felt that this was a very surprising phone call, as the reasons she stated were very weak. However, we were not surprised that Ms. Cikos had found a reason to reject our case. In our face-to-face meeting with Ms. Cikos, she was unwilling to learn anything about us or even to hear anything we had to say. When we made a cry for help by calling someone else and trying to find other agencies, we felt that this represented to Ms. Cikos the opportunity she had been looking for, albeit weak, to finally reject our case, as she had been wanting to all along.

Our assumptions about Ms. Cikos could have been completely erroneous; however, Walter voiced this concern to Ms. Cikos by stating during this phone call on January 23, "From the beginning, when you met with us in person, you were ready to let us go," to which Ms. Cikos replied, "Yes, I was."

In summary, without ever having met us, and without ever getting a proper update of our case, Ms. Shawna Cikos formed the resolution that she did not want us to be clients of West Coast Child and Family Services. This resolution has caused us to believe that there were other, personal reasons for Ms. Cikos's desire to reject our case.

5) During our phone conversation with Ms. Cikos on January 23, the two reasons she stated to us for no longer wanting to handle our case were (1) we had emailed Phyllis Greenberg, and (2) we had looked for another place to do a home study. Reason number one has been addressed above, and was addressed in the letter that we received today, dated February 8. Regarding Ms. Cikos's second reason, we were completely shocked and puzzled by this reason to discontinue our case.

We never had any indication that, while we were working with West Coast Child and Family Services, we were not allowed to look for referrals from other agencies. In fact, as mentioned previously, Ms. Cikos had told us several times in our meeting on January 22 that, if we weren't happy, we should go to another agency.

If it was not illegal for us to look for referrals for other agencies, then it should not have been a reason to reject our case. If we were not allowed to look for referrals, then Ms. Cikos should not have encouraged us to do so.

In either case, Ms. Cikos told us repeatedly that she would clearly state, in a letter to us, her two reasons for closing our case; she included one of the reasons (emailing Ms. Greenberg), but neglected to include her second reason (looking for referrals for other agencies). We would like to have a new letter created and submitted to us via US Mail including Ms. Cikos's second reason for rejecting our case.

The deep, heartfelt longing to bring a child into a family is something that an agency like yours should understand, and our pleas for help should have been dealt with using understanding and patience.

The experiences we have gone through since January 22 have brought about sorrow of the most acute kind, second only to the death of our twins. Our attempts to bring this situation to a resolution before losing the possibility to adopt yet another child should have been understood by your agency and all of your workers. West Coast Child and Family Services has shown a grave lack of compassion for the dreams and heartaches of families, indicating to us that West Coast Child and Family Services is working hard to keep children out of good homes.

It is now clear to us that no one at West Coast Child and Family Services is willing to communicate with us properly in order to complete a home study. This home study process was conducted with miscommunications, misrepresentations, preconceived and unbendable ideas on the part of West Coast Child and Family Services, complete absence of compassion, unprofessional and childish conduct on the part of its employees, and total unwillingness to consider the role that West Coast has played in the failure of this home study. Therefore, our desired outcome is not to make an appeal to be allowed to continue working with West Coast Child and Family Services. As our desire to have an additional child become part of our household is clearly not the common goal of West Coast Child and Family Services, our second choice is to have the $2,000.00 that we paid to you returned to us. As a result of West Coast Child and Family Services' disinclination to give us the opportunity for a proper home study, we believe that this payment was never used by West Coast Child and Family Services with the appropriate purposes for which it was intended, and we would, therefore, like to have the funds returned to us.

As we have had a severe communication problem from everyone at West Coast Child and Family Services, we have decided to be proactive; if you do not respond to this letter within 5 working days, we will move on to Step II in the West Coast Child and Family Services' Grievance Procedures process, with the following steps taken after additional 5-day periods elapse.

Sincerely,
Walter and Sarah Cavilry

cc: Shawna Cikos
Violet Coolidge

I sealed up my composition, put it in an envelope, and, with a satisfied, smug grin on my face, mailed the letter off to West Coast. Onward.

* * *

The following day, after a couple of Google searches and much relief, I found a new adoption agency, The Adoption Center in the west side area of Los Angeles. Walter and I soon met with Destiny at TAC, a very sweet woman with shoulder-length, straight, light-brown hair, a blue business suit, and experience with Down syndrome adoption. I was relieved on many levels.

As my letter to West Coast was, that morning, beginning its trek across Los Angeles, I went to a coffee shop to sit and relax while sipping on a venti. I brought along my laptop to outline and organize some of the paperwork for our second attempt at a home study. Although I felt like I was becoming a bit of an expert at all this filling-out and collecting, the second round of home studying was no less an arduous assignment than the first.

My current bureaucratic burden caused me to speculate—Shawna had, with our official rejection letter, returned our photos and marriage certificate duplicates—why hadn't she returned anything else? There were doctors' reports, letters, and numerous papers that, if I had them, I could pass on to TAC, eliminating a lot of time, work, and waste.

Mentally empowered by the eight-page novella heading toward West Coast, I emailed Shawna from my laptop, with a carbon copy to Violet.

Hi Shawna,

We received the envelope you sent to us, which included two items from our file:

1) a copy of our marriage certificate
2) our family photos.

At this time, we're ready to have the rest of the items from our file sent to us, including but not limited to:

1) medical report from Sarah's doctor
2) medical report from Walter's doctor
3) medical report from Heidi's doctor
4) letter from Walter's therapist
5) various letters of recommendation
6) Sarah's employment verification
7) Walter's employment verification

Thank you so much!
Sarah Cavilry

Six minutes later, mid sip of venti drip, I heard the ding of email received. It was from Violet and said, succinctly, "Oh, Really!"

Reading this, I audibly chuckled. The lack of professionalism was comedic. With a new agency on our side, I felt like a body builder getting ready to kick a foot-full of sand up the nose of a wimp. I responded to Violet immediately.

Hi Violet,

From your response, I am assuming that I did the wrong thing in asking for other items from my file. Please let me know if I have misinterpreted your response.

As we were returned two items from the file, we wondered if we could have other items as well. If we're not allowed the other items, please feel free to tell me so, as we are unaware of the rules.

My only request is that we be allowed to make our final transactions with West Coast in as calm and professional a manner as possible.

Thank you very much for your understanding in this matter.

Sarah Cavilry

I patted myself on the back, buffed my fingernails on my chest, and gave myself a good-buddy punch in the chin. Then I clicked send. I received no emailed or snail-mailed response.

Mere days ago, I was a blubbering, depressed heap, but I'd quickly evolved into my personal version of a superwoman.

Chapter 12:

Him

A few weeks into a brand new home study process, I received a voicemail message from Robin in Cincinnati. I had been waiting to hear an update on the unborn baby girl.

Robin's message said, "I was waiting to get a concrete decision from the birth parents before calling you. I didn't want to give you incomplete information. Well, they've finally made a decision, and they want to parent the baby themselves rather than give her up." Peacefully, I listened to the closing comments of her message before she thanked us for our understanding and hung up the phone.

The little girl's parents had decided to keep her. Well, she was a very lucky little girl, and her parents had made a great decision. Although I had a brief, fleeting moment of, "Aw, darn…" I knew the right decision had been made. That baby girl would have a loving mom and dad, and Walter and I could start fresh on our home study without the pressure of any time constraints. Mentally, I wished that tiny baby the most incredible life ever, and, with a smile, I watched as life's road thus made a turn.

For the next three months, I proceeded with the hefty paperwork process involved in this second home study. Shawna had replied to me with a letter, but had only believed it appropriate to return four pieces of paperwork to me—Walter's and my doctor's reports, and Walter's and my employment verifications. That still left me with a lot of work to do. So be it. I rolled up my sleeves and prepared to do what needed to be done.

Shawna had also returned $1,500 to us, minus a $500 application fee. Not too shabby. When that check came in, I decided to mentally detach myself from West Coast—I didn't want to pursue a corrected rejection letter or any kind of disciplinary action against Violet or

Shawna for their childish unprofessionalism, or against Eliza for impeding our ability to adopt. Attempting to work with that agency had been the most frustrating, illogical, and emotionally painful experience of my life, and I didn't want to revisit it. I just wanted to forget about the nightmare that was West Coast Child and Family Services. Life's path was leading me somewhere much nicer than the dirt road where West Coast resided, and I didn't want to make a return trip.

While we were finishing collecting documents and scheduling interviews with Tina, our very professional and understanding TAC social worker, I got a call at work from Robin in Cincinnati. A baby boy with Down syndrome had been born in San Francisco three days previously, and he was available for adoption. When I told her we were interested, she let me know that a lawyer would be calling shortly.

Less than an hour later, I got a call from Pauline, an adoption attorney in northern California.

"So, you're interested in adopting the baby boy with Down syndrome, right?"

"Yes," I informed her exuberantly, "we're very interested."

Pauline began, "Well, let me tell you a little bit about the situation. The birth parents didn't know the baby had Down's, so they gave him up at the hospital. The baby boy is three days old, and he has bright red hair."

I felt a wave of emotion shoot through me. I suppressed the urge to think, "I've found my baby." But I did excitedly respond, "I have red hair, too!"

"I know! That's what Robin told me!" We oohed and giggled together like high school girl in the locker room talking about a cute boy.

Pauline went on. "The birth parents would like an open adoption. Are you okay with that?"

Walter and I wanted a new baby to have access to medical and personal information as well as a possible relationship with the birth parents, so I answered, "Yes, we definitely want that."

"Great. Oh, and the baby has the heart defect that a lot of Down's babies have. Is that okay?"

The chance of a baby with Down syndrome also being born with heart disease is about 50/50, so we had already talked about that possibility and decided that we would accept a baby with additional medical problems as well. "Yeah, Walter and I are okay with that."

Pauline made her concluding statement: "So, after hearing about the whole situation, are you still interested?"

With excitement mounting, I said, "Very interested."

"Okay, then," Pauline instructed me, "Do you have a 'Dear Birth Parents' letter?"

I didn't, but, completely undeterred, I let her know I could write one in 15 minutes.

"Great," she went on. "I also need a family picture...do you have one?"

On my computer, I had a digital copy of the picture Shawna had rejected and returned. "Yeah, I do."

"Perfect," Pauline concluded. "Email the letter and picture to me as soon as you can—my office closes at 5:00."

It was 4:15. Without hesitation, I blurted out, "No problem. I'll get it to you before then." Pauline gave me her email address, and we hung up our phones.

I ran to my desk computer and began composing.

Dear Birth Parents,

Thank you so much for reading this letter in order to learn a little bit about our family. This is probably a very difficult time for you, and we wish you all the best during this period. Please let us tell you a little bit about ourselves.

We are Walter, Sarah, and Heidi. We live in a household which is full of love, laughter, and understanding; our constant desire is to make certain that our home and family is a place of safety and comfort for all of us, especially 5-year-old Heidi. We love our family!

We believe strongly in the importance of our family unit: spending time together, communicating, playing and telling each other how much we love each other. The fact that we believe so strongly in the strength of our family helps us deal with life's challenges.

Walter and Sarah met at the community college where we both work. Walter is very popular at our workplace for being extremely helpful, friendly, caring, and funny; he's famous all over campus, which makes Sarah very proud! People who know Walter are always telling Sarah stories of how he has helped them at work or in their personal lives; he truly enjoys helping people. Walter has a great sense of humor and is always making people laugh. The one thing that Sarah likes about Walter most is, if he sees a stranger on the street that seems to need help, he always offers to help. Sarah has learned that quality from him and now she always tries to do that as well.

Sarah is somewhat shy, so she tries to overcompensate for that by having a big smile for people she sees. Sarah really enjoys interacting with people, being friendly, and making people smile or laugh. A strength of Sarah's is her caring attitude toward other people and her desire to help.

Heidi is a very beautiful, caring, sensitive, smart, and funny girl. She loves to play with children of any age, from the babies at her preschool/daycare to her best friend who is 5 years older than her; she gets along with kids of all ages. Heidi's specialty is making babies laugh. If we're at a restaurant and a baby is crying, Heidi will take it upon herself to play peek-a-boo with the baby until the cries are replaced with laughter. Heidi truly adores children, and she desperately wants to be a big sister. Heidi is extremely loving and sensitive. If she sees a movie or goes to a play and there is a sad song, she'll start to cry. Sarah and Walter love Heidi's sensitivity and ability to be compassionate at such a young age.

We spend Fridays with Walter's mother, and we vary weekend days between family and friends, enjoying whichever events we can take in. Sometimes the day's activity is a play, a movie, the park, or the backyard. Sometimes it's just a walk around the block visiting neighbors, or listening to the frogs in the nearby wash. We like to keep an open mind to whatever comes our way.

In preparing our daughter for a new addition to the family, we have talked to Heidi about how the baby won't come out of mommy's tummy, but someone will help us bring the baby into our family. We hope to adopt a baby with Down syndrome, so we have been bringing Heidi to participate in activities where people with different disabilities will be present, such as a recent version of "Seussical, the Musical" presented by "Pine Theatre for Everyone", which included many cast members with Down syndrome. Yesterday, we took Heidi to a playground at "Old Valley Center", which is a local school that provides services for children with developmental disabilities.

Walter and Sarah have always felt the need to do something important for someone else during our lifetimes. Sarah has always had a strong connection with people who are disabled, especially people who have Down syndrome. She has been working with disabled people ever since she was 16 years old. Presently, Sarah works as a sign language interpreter, and she plans on teaching sign language to a new baby, just as she taught sign language to Heidi (sign language is often taught to children with Down syndrome, as speech can sometimes be difficult).

As Sarah works in the Student Resources Center at a community college, she has vast amounts of access to information on services for children with Down syndrome; Sarah's friends are all people in helping professions, so they are very excited for us and ready to help out with resources we might need. If we ever come across a situation we don't know how to handle, we have people to ask for advice. Adopting a child with a disability is going to be a challenge, but because of our knowledgeable friends and colleagues, and because of Sarah's long history of working with people who have Down syndrome, the challenge is one we feel ready to face. [I wrote that last sentence and the one about Seussical the Musical because of our conversations with Eliza. I was still worried that it was not considered acceptable to be excited about a child with Down syndrome. The shock over working with West Coast hadn't worn off yet.]

Thank you so much for taking the time to read our letter, and for considering us as adoptive parents. We truly hope that, amidst this difficult choice you have to make, we can help you feel that you have made a good choice by selecting our family.

Very sincerely,
Walter, Sarah, and Heidi

I forwarded the letter to Walter's email address and called him, ordering him to open it immediately, make any necessary changes or edits, and return it to me at once. He did as he was told.

I pasted the letter into the body of a new email, attached our family picture, and sent the collaboration off to Pauline, who immediately responded, "You have an adorable family." I felt pretty good about The Cavilrys at that moment, too.

And I had gotten the job done by 4:45.

* * *

Walter and I decided we would wait to hear word from the lawyer before mentioning the potential baby brother to Heidi. We ended up having to keep the secret for a very short time—Pauline called me on my cell phone at 10:30 the next morning.

She said, slowly and slyly, "Sarah...?"

My eyes opened as wide as they could go without actually popping out of my skull. My heart jumped in my chest. "What? What?" I held my breath while Pauline said words I had been longing to hear. "The parents chose you."

The parents chose you.

I wanted to jump up and scream, to release all the tension that had been building for the past two years. But after so many false starts and disappointments, I was afraid to celebrate. Did the phrase, *the parents chose you*, really mean what it sounded like? Were they going to relinquish their baby to us? Were we going to have him in our home? Was I going to raise him? Would Heidi be his big sister? Would Walter and I watch him go to his first day of kindergarten and his last day of high school? I was watching my future flash before my eyes. Rather than continue to wonder, I asked for clarification.

"Can I be excited?"

Pauline laughed. "Yes, you should be very excited now."

Clutching the cell phone to my ear, I ran outside of my office with a huge smile on my face and tears blurring my path, saying nothing more than a repeated, "Oh my god. Oh my god."

While I gathered my senses, Pauline let me know, "You need to hop in the car and head to UC San Francisco right now—the baby is there alone."

I collected my thoughts, collected my husband and daughter, filled up the gas tank, and began the six-hour trek to meet our fourth and final family member, a red-headed baby boy.

* * *

The transition from work to journey was bustling and immediate. Quite suddenly, we were on the road to northern California.

As we started down the freeway onramp, Heidi asked innocently and with nonchalance, "Where are we going?" I wondered why it hadn't, until now, struck her as unusual that we were picking her up only a couple of hours after dropping her off.

I had thought about this moment for a while and mentally rehearsed what I thought appropriate to say.

In California, when a child is relinquished to adoptive parents, the birth parents are allowed a 30-day period during which they can change their minds and take the baby back. Tina had told us the story of a little boy who brought his newly adopted baby brother to first-grade show-and-tell only to have the birth parents take the baby back before the 30 day deadline. With that story in mind, I answered Heidi's question.

"Well, we found out about a baby that has no parents. We are going to help that baby by keeping him at our house for a little while and taking care of him. We're going to a hospital to pick him up, and then he'll come home with us for a little while."

After a beat, I glanced at Walter and whispered, "Are you okay with that?"

He replied pleasantly but with conviction, "Actually, I'm not okay with that. I don't think we should lie to her. She's five years old now and she's smart. I think she can understand the truth."

I felt a bit silly for not having run my idea by Walter before saying it to Heidi. But with Walter's okay, I actually felt relieved. Telling Heidi the truth would be easier than keeping up a lie for 30 days. And telling the truth felt like a better way to start out the relationship with her prospective baby brother.

I turned around and looked at Heidi, who was quietly playing with a Barbie doll in the back seat.

"Heidi, what I told you about the baby—that wasn't actually true."

She looked up from Barbie. "There isn't a baby?"

"There is a baby, but we're actually hoping to adopt him and make him your brother."

"Really?"

"Yeah. But while he's with us, for 30 whole days, the mother who gave birth to him is allowed to decide if she wants to take him back."

"Oh."

"So he'll be with us, but if the mother wants him back, we have to give him back."

"That's stupid."

"Well, it's the rule. I just want to make sure you understand. If 30 days goes by, then we get to keep him forever."

"Well, if he's not really ours yet, can I still hold him?"

I smiled. "Of course. You can hold him as much as you want." I knew, with this child or any other, she was going to be a great big sister.

Once we settled onto the freeway, GPS navigating the way to the UCSF Hospital, I made the first of many necessary phone calls. Number one on the list was Mom. We instructed her to get a plane ticket and meet us in San Francisco—we'd pick her up at the airport. We also gave her a verbal list of things we needed her to bring from our home: phone chargers, tooth brushes, clothes and under-things. If there was anything else we needed, we'd buy it in San Francisco. She hung up and got to work, excited to meet her potential grandson.

While preparing to make the next phone call, I asked Walter,

"What do you think of the name Phillip?"

He made only brief consideration before replying, "I like Phillip. That's a nice name."

After the struggle Walter and I had gone through with naming Heidi, I was pleased that this particular naming was controversy-free. This gave me the courage to continue the naming quest.

"And I'd like to include my dad's name in there, too. Can we name the baby Phillip Jonathon?"

Having once told Walter that I would like to name a future son after my father, he had responded that he wasn't in favor of pressuring a child to live up to a certain reputation, and that's what he believed being a namesake conveyed. However, having had a very different childhood experience from Walter's, I consider naming a child after a beloved relative the greatest possible honor, rather than a burden, and I wanted very much to do this for my father.

But unexpectedly, Walter responded with the counter offer, "What about Jonathon Phillip?"

Up went the red flag. It has been my experience that Walter, when he doesn't necessarily want something that he believes someone else wants, will try to overcompensate by giving the requestor more than is asked for. For example, I might tell Walter I'm craving a big pizza for dinner, and the next thing I know, I find myself at an expensive Italian restaurant wearing my best clothes when all the both of us really wanted was to wear our pajamas and pig out on Domino's in front of the television. He goes overboard to please, often to the dissatisfaction of all involved.

In the case of naming our new baby, Walter's offer to change the ordering from "Phillip Jonathon" to "Jonathon Phillip" led me to believe that he thought I wanted our new son to have the go-by-the-middle-name format that my mother, daughter, stepfather, and I all utilize. Mom's legal name is Sarah Alexandra, but everyone calls her "Alex". My stepfather's first name is Ashley, but he is known by his middle name's diminutive form, Rob (good choice.) Everyone calls me Sarah, but the name on my birth certificate is Rufina Sarah-Jane. To continue the tradition, we named our daughter Rose-Sarah Heidi. As a result, Heidi's full name shares the R-initial first name with mine, the hyphen from my Sarah-Jane, and the Sarah from my mom's Sarah Alexandra. Although a lot of fun for our first offspring, I had gotten that kind of creative confusion out of my system; it really wasn't necessary to assign that burden to our next kid.

"We don't have to do that again. I don't need all of our kids to go by their middle name."

With total honesty, Walter explained with an embarrassed giggle, "But Jonathon Phillip sounds better than Phillip Jonathon."

I thought to myself, "Then we'd *really* be naming the baby after my dad." Also, Jonathon Phillip was, truly, a nicer combination.

"I'd like that," I decided. I dialed my dad.

When he picked up the phone, I said, "Hey Dad, guess where we're going."

He responded with his typical what-are-you-up-to-now tone, "*Where?*"

"We're heading to San Francisco to pick up a baby boy."

In his usual way, he was reservedly excited as well as nervous about his daughter's newest adventure. "Oh my goodness, how exciting! Good luck." He asked the usual questions about when we would see the baby and when we would bring him home. And what we would name him.

"We've decided on Phillip."

Dad responded with content approval. "Phillip? That's a nice name."

"We're going to call him Phillip," I went on, "but that's actually going to be his middle name. His first name will be Jonathon."

My dad's voice went up half an octave and instantly began to crack. "Oh, wow! That's great!" He paused for breath before saying, "I always thought about someone being named after me, but I never knew it would mean so much." In the background, I heard my step-mom playfully yell, "Are you making my husband cry?" It felt good to have given my dad the joy that brought him to tears.

* * *

At 5:00 PM, we pulled up in front of the airport just as Mom was coming out of the baggage area—plans were running smoothly already. By 6:00 we pulled into the parking lot of the hotel local to the UCSF Hospital. Pauline was going to meet us there, then walk us to the Neonatal Intensive Care Unit to meet Phillip. Mom quickly checked our family into the hotel while Walter and I gathered up Heidi and brought her into the hotel lobby. Key cards in hand, we went up the elevator to our second-floor room.

The drive must have been long and difficult for Heidi. The hours were tiring for Walter and me, but for a five-year-old girl, that kind of boring sitting around is comparable to torture. So, within the exciting new confines of our hotel room, our daughter released a bit of that pent up energy. Immediately inside, Heidi got up on one of the two queen-size beds and began jumping repeatedly from mattress to mattress, taking a running start from the far edge of one, vaulting, and landing again and again on the other, laughing loudly all the while. After she tired of that, she asked dad to sit on one bed and stretch his legs out to touch the other mattress so that she could walk across his body like a bridge. Their plan wasn't very successful, but they certainly tried (God forbid Walter should say *no* to such a request from his precious girl.)

We had planned to meet with Pauline outside the hotel at 7:30 PM. When that hour arrived, we gathered ourselves up and went to an outdoor seating area in front of the hotel's café. My little girl, after her post-traveled bed-bouncing exercise, was ready for some dinner. Walter took her into the café to see what they served that a tired five-year-old might actually eat. I walked them into the restaurant to help Walter make a meal choice, then left the two of them inside to wait for grilled cheese while I looked for Pauline.

When I turned away from the door to face the white-plastic-chair-and-table bedecked courtyard of the hotel, there was a woman standing in front of me. She was tall, 30-ish, and very beautiful with a striking resemblance to Scarlett Johansson.

"Sarah?" she asked.

I responded with the premonition of being taken, mere minutes from now, to meet my baby boy. Excitement bubbled over and became evident in my excessively energetic tone. I hadn't even met my son yet, but I already wanted to celebrate.

"Yes! Are you Pauline?"

"No…I'm Loretta."

It was the birth mother.

I think the word "awkward" could be defined by the environment at that moment, this young woman and me, staring at each other, not knowing whether to shake hands, hug, cry, or run. The only reaction I could think of was to say, "Oh," smile, and pat her on the arm. I prayed for the world's most speedily grilled grilled-cheese so that Walter could save me from my inept ability to make adequate, appropriate conversation with the woman whose baby I was taking.

Wasn't the baby supposed to be alone? I secretly wished for his abandonment.

Luckily, out walked Mom to, unbeknownst to her, help me with chitchat. When I introduced them to each other, Mom shook Loretta's hand with a smile and a bubbly, "It's so nice to meet you!" A young man walked up with a woman in her 50s, and Loretta introduced the two as her husband, Mike, and her mom, Betsy. We all shook hands and passed around smiles, but I longed for the presence of Pauline to act as an experienced mediator for this uncomfortably surreal event.

We seated ourselves in the flimsy molded-plastic chairs and made ourselves as comfortable as possible, looking at each other, discomfited smiles glued to our faces. Gratefully, Walter and Heidi joined us, after what seemed like hours, toting a Styrofoam to-go box of grilled cheese with fries, which my daughter happily munched. Immediately thereafter, I saw a middle-aged, casually dressed and pleasant looking blonde woman bound across the parking lot and over to our tables. Her immediate ability to mediate the uncomfortable adoption situation and ease tensions told me that she must be Pauline.

"I'm sorry it took me so long to get here. Have you all met each other?"

I was glad to have someone there who was experienced with this kind of touchy, emotional meeting. Pauline asked Loretta and Mike how their drives to San Francisco were (their baby had been transported to a specialized hospital, 45 minutes from their home hospital, shortly after the Down syndrome was identified), asked where Betsy had traveled from, and offered my mom similar questions. Although I was still nervous, the atmosphere immediately lightened.

Then, at a pause in the niceties, Loretta spoke.

"Well, Sarah, I have something for you."

From behind her seat at the table, she pulled out a very large gift bag, almost as tall as my hip, decorated with blue cartoon teddy bears and, in big block letters, the familiar phrase, "It's a Boy!" It was so huge, but my emotional ill ease must have kept me from noticing it before it was presented to me formally.

Looking at the package, I surmised that it had probably come from her baby shower. My feelings of self-consciousness were recharged.

I began looking through the items in the big gift bag. There were toys, bottles, pacifiers, and clothes—so many clothes—so small, so boyish, so blue. Clearly, Loretta and her friends knew she was going to have a little boy.

"And I have something for you, Heidi."

Loretta handed a small gift bag to my daughter. Inside, carefully wrapped in pink tissue paper, was a T-shirt with red script on the front which read, "I'm the Big Sister". What a nice person Loretta is, I thought, that she would consider Heidi's joy as well as my own. I had a weird, vivid image flash in my mind of Loretta in Target, stone-faced, looking for a shirt for Heidi. Recently post-childbirth, I wonder if she was tired or sore while she shopped. I never wondered if she was sad.

Pauline made a little more small talk and presented us with a few forms to sign before she finally asked,

"Well, should we all walk to the hospital?"

Sitting, talking, signing, and getting acquainted, all the while I had been waiting impatiently to get to the hospital to meet my little baby son. Now, we finally all stood to begin our walk to the UC San Francisco NICU. If I had thought it appropriate, I would have run.

As we began our stroll, I noticed that Mom and Betsy had fallen behind the group, walking slowly and having a long, unpausing conversation. I made a note to ask Mom later what they had been talking about.

After what felt like miles of journeying, turns right and left and long stretches of road, I finally saw, towering in front of me, a multi-story beige brick building with "UC San Francisco" across the front in burgundy Helvetica. When we entered the hospital lobby, Loretta knew where to go, and led the group to the NICU waiting room. Again, fleetingly, I wondered, *I thought the baby was in the hospital alone.* When I saw how familiar Loretta was with her surroundings, I assumed that I had misunderstood. But, inwardly, I wished again, especially right now, that the baby had been abandoned after birth; then I wouldn't have had to go through the uncomfortable awkwardness associated with this otherwise 100% joyous event.

At the NICU front desk, Pauline introduced our group to the attendant.

"The adoptive parents would like to go in to meet their new baby."

Walter and I followed Loretta and Mike through the double doors that led into the NICU. A few feet into the hallway, I stopped. This was the ultimate moment before seeing my son for the first time, and I wanted to make sure I did it right.

"Walter, is it okay with you if Mom goes in with me first?"

When Heidi was born, we had planned for months that my mom would be present at the birth. However, due to a few medical complications and a very annoying nurse, my mom was instructed to wait in the lobby, causing her to be absent for the crucial moment. I never stopped feeling guilty about that, and had longed for the day when I could make it up to her. This was the perfect opportunity.

Knowing exactly what I had in mind, Walter responded, "I think that's a great idea." He went out to get my mom, but returned immediately, saying, "She won't come. She says I should go first."

But I was adamant. "Then tell her I'm not going in without her."

While waiting for the return of Walter or the appearance of my mom, Loretta asked, "Are you planning on changing his name? You can keep the name we chose, or you can change it. It doesn't matter to me." I really didn't like the trendy-sounding and common name she had chosen, Caden, so I was very glad that she didn't mind me choosing an alternative.

When I told her we planned on calling the baby Phillip, she asked, "Oh, is that a family name?"

"No, we just like it." I was a little embarrassed by this conversation, the admission that we were rejecting the name she had chosen.

I noted a small roll of the eye—she seemed not to like our name choice so much either. But she said, "Oh, well, that's okay. You can name him whatever you want. I don't care."

Finally, my mom entered the hallway. I was relieved that Mom had decided to let me have my way. Now, Loretta, Mike, Mom and I headed silently into the NICU.

I saw several isolets with newborn babies lying swaddled inside the clear plastic-walled units, most of the tiny infants burdened with numerous tubes and connected to monitors, some with a parent or two by their side.

A nurse walked up to Loretta and welcomed her, calling her by name. The nurse then, shifting her friendly gaze to meet mine, asked, "Are you adopting the baby?"

Cheerfully and with great excitement, I responded, "Yes!"

The nurse welcomed Mom and I with a smile and said, "The baby has a little jaundice, so he's under some billi lights right now. But here he is."

There had been a sudden and rapid onslaught of activity since last night's call from Robin in Cincinnati, but this one moment felt like I had reached the end of a long, difficult voyage, like Tom Hanks on his raft with Wilson, and I had finally seen a ship.

We were led to an isolet on the end of a row. Lying there, body unblanketed under the comfortable warmth of the billi lights, was a little pink baby, big blue eye shades covering his face from forehead to cheekbone, and a tuft of bright orange hair standing straight up from his tiny head.

The nurse reached behind the boy's head and unfastened the eye mask. Pulling the cover away, I saw the sleeping eyes of my baby boy—and they were the beautiful almond-shaped eyes of an angel with Down syndrome. A journey that had started back in my Spanish dancing days, through my first job, alongside every child I met with Down syndrome, and with the rocky trails toward adoption had come to an end at this moment. I was at the bedside of the child I had longed for—he was right in front of me—and I couldn't contain my joy.

I burst into tears. Life's road had many twists and turns, but ended here, and it was the perfect destination.

The nurse smiled, "Would you like to hold him?"

I collected myself and said, "Absolutely."

"You can sit in the chair right behind you." There was a large rocking chair next to the isolet. I picked up the pillow on the seat and said, "Mom, you sit down."

She looked at me, shocked. "But you should hold him first."

"No," I said with defiance, "you're going to be the first person to hold him." She tried to give a response of refusal, but one more, "No, sit," was all she needed to be convinced. She therefore sat, put a pillow on her lap, and welcomed her tiny grandson into her arms.

We looked and touched, cooed and giggled. Loretta used the lawyer's camera to take pictures. Mike stood to the side, stoically silent. After a few minutes, Mike left the room and sent Walter in with Heidi so we could all meet Phillip together. Walter walked into the NICU accompanied by Heidi who, upon first sighting of her baby brother, let loose an enormous, involuntary "Aww!" of delight, a little too loud for a hospital room full of sleeping babies, necessitating a stereo, "Shh!" from both Mom and Dad. Heidi gave us a little preview of life to come. She touched and kissed Phillip so much that we wondered how he got enough oxygen into his lungs with Heidi in such close proximity, sucking up all his air.

Mom enjoyed her grandmotherly moment to satisfaction before she said, "Would you like to hold him now?"

Without pause, I exploded, "Yes!" I think I even clapped.

The nurse took the little redhead from my mom's arms, juggling cords and tubes like an expert. When mom's hands were free, she hugged me and whispered in my ear, "Thank you. That meant so much to me."

"Of course, Mommy." Both of us content, Mom found her way out of the NICU.

Now it was my turn. When I made myself comfortable in the provided rocking chair, that beautiful baby was presented to me. He was so soft and warm and so tiny. He fit perfectly into my arms and felt so good there. I looked over every inch of his face—his peaceful eyes, his teeny tiny nose, his heart-shaped pink lips, his small, round ears, and the bright orange tuft of hair which stuck straight up on top of his head. I ran my fingers through his hair again and again, making it poke straight up, lay back down, part left, part right, and straight up again. I took pictures of him with my cell phone and sent them to family and friends (My friend Billie quickly responded, "He looks just like Beaker from The Muppet Show!" I had to admit she was right.) I looked at his little fingers, resisting the urge to unwrap his swaddled blanket and look at his tiny toes. I felt the warmth of peace and contentment run through my veins as, for the first time, I cradled my baby boy—my Phillip—in my arms.

Walter leaned over my shoulder to examine facial features, just as I was. Heidi stood in front of me, touching Phillip's miniature fingers again and again, putting her hands on his cheeks again and again...and again. I was able to convince Heidi to stop groping the baby long enough to stand by my side and smile at the nurse, who snapped a picture of our family of four.

When I finally decided I could relinquish my hold long enough to let Walter have a turn, the nurse took Phillip from me, saying,

"Maybe we should change his diaper first. Would anyone like to change him?"

"I would," Loretta requested, looking at me and adding, "Is that okay?"

"Oh, of course!" I assured her. I was surprised and touched that she felt a desire to have a moment of connection with the baby she had created.

Heidi and I stood at the foot of the isolet, a few feet away from Loretta and the nurse, as they busily manipulated diapers, wipes and talc. When the wet diaper had been removed and Phillip's little bottom was getting some fresh air, Heidi leaned over to me and whispered, "He has a very cute little privates." I giggled and put my arm around her shoulder. "Yes, he does," I agreed.

Loretta's two-and-a-half year old son, Freddie, had been left in the care of a babysitter, and Heidi was getting tired after this very long day. Walter took a few moments to experience and enjoy holding Phillip before we decided it was time to go our separate ways, us to the hotel, Loretta's family members to their homes. I gave Phillip several good-bye hugs before finally leaving the hospital.

While recharging our emotional and physical batteries through the power of room service, I remembered to ask Mom what she and Betsy had been discussing during the walk to the hospital. Apparently, Betsy quite enjoys talking, and since Mom is rather an aficionado of listening to and processing gossip, the two grandmothers made a great pair.

Betsy had told Mom a little about Loretta's pregnancy.

Loretta's doctor had given the parents the option of having a diagnostic test done to find out if her unborn baby had Down syndrome, but a neighbor was certain that the test was undesirable and unnecessary. The procedure carries with it some risks to the unborn baby, including the possibility of spontaneous miscarriage. Additionally, as Loretta was healthy, athletic, and young—only 27— her baby most likely wouldn't have Down syndrome anyway, as the neighbor explained to her.

So, the decision was made to forego the diagnostic procedure. For Phillip's sake, that was a lucky decision indeed; if the test had been performed and the Down syndrome discovered, Betsy informed my mother, Loretta would have certainly terminated the pregnancy.

A shiver went through me, and I sighed with tremendous relief that we had met and held Phillip.

Chapter 13:

Turns

Early the next morning while Mom and Walter continued to snooze, I felt a little girl's morning-breath in my face.

"Mom. Mom."

I slowly opened my eyes to find myself nose-to-nose with Heidi, who was standing at my bedside.

With a groan, I mumbled, "What?"

"Let's go see the baby."

I rubbed my eyes, blinked, and propped myself up on one elbow. Whispering, I responded, "Honey, I don't want to wake Daddy up. He's really tired from the drive yesterday."

Ignorant of my complete lack of a sense of direction and disregarding the lengthy walk from the hotel to the hospital, she offered, "We don't have to wake Daddy up. Just me and you can go."

"Honey, I don't know how to get there by myself."

"But I know how."

The last thing in the world I felt like doing at 6:30 in the morning in a strange town was getting lost. I insisted, "Honey, I just can't."

But Heidi insisted as well. "No, Mommy, I know how to get there."

"Heidi, I don't know…"

"Mom, I know how to get there. Really. Come on." And she started toward the door.

Slowly, I got out of bed. I thought, even though I don't know how to navigate the streets to the hospital and the hallways to the NICU, I could at least go outside with Heidi to let her get out of the room, walk in a square block around the hotel building and allow Walter and Mom to sleep in a bit. After hastily dressing, Heidi and I stepped out of our hotel room and into the corridor.

I was already lost.

As someone with a very poor sense of space and location, I always make sure to take in my surroundings visually to construct a map in my brain of the layout. Standing in front of the closed door, I looked left and right, creating mental photographs of the walls, doors, and windows in order to ensure a greater chance of making my eventual return to the room. Before I could decide which way to go, Heidi chirped, "Come on!" and started walking. Rather than worry about whether or not she had chosen the correct path, I decided to go ahead and let her lead the way. I continued to take note of everything I passed, looking behind me often to see what would be in front of us when we came back. That way, I could freely allow Heidi to stroll and explore the building; then, when she became hopelessly lost, I could guide her back to our room.

Luckily, Heidi was able to accurately lead us to the elevator, the lobby, and out of the building—at least we'd get some fresh air. She headed to the left and down the sidewalk while I followed in silence, looking at buildings, signs, greenery, and other landmarks surrounding me, but when we crossed the street and made a turn, I got confused.

"Heidi, I'm lost. Maybe we should go back and wait for Daddy to wake up."

"No, Daddy needs to sleep. He's tired from driving yesterday. I know where to go."

She was leading me with such confidence that, momentarily, I wondered if she would actually be able to get me to the hospital. Snapping myself out of that fantasy, I remembered that I had my phone in my pocket; if need be, I could call a cab.

Heidi and I walked, her pace a foot ahead of mine, down and across street after street. Looking up to add the sign on the next building to my inner photo album, I found myself standing beneath the UC San Francisco Hospital front entrance.

We went in the double glass doors and I headed to the reception desk to ask for directions to the NICU, but Heidi passed me right by and walked confidently down a corridor. After a momentary pause, I told the reception volunteer, "Never mind," and followed my daughter; she had brought me this far—why not see how much farther she could go? Sure enough, Heidi showed me the way to the elevator, pushed the button for the correct floor, directed me to the NICU, through more double doors, around various babies in isolets, and to the bedside of her sleeping baby brother.

After an hour and a half of holding and diapering and feeding, Walter called me on my cell phone.

"Where are you guys?"

"Heidi brought me to the hospital."

Knowing well my directional impairments, and referring to his own exceptional skills, he laughed, "That's my girl."

I have since learned that when Heidi says, "Mom, I'm sure," I should believe her.

* * *

Phillip, although basically healthy, needed to remain in the hospital until he could drink a full two-ounce bottle of formula within half an hour. His Down syndrome caused general low muscle tone, making the suction required for bottle feeding a tiring task for his tiny cheeks. One of the nurses taught us a very interesting bottle-feeding technique to assist weak little babies, like Phillip, who weren't strong enough to get a good latch on a nipple.

I would lay Phillip's two-ounce bottle in the crook between my thumb and index fingers and gently put the nipple in his mouth. I would then use the tips of my thumb and middle finger of the same hand to push inward on his cheeks. This would, somehow, give him the added suction necessary to get milk out of the bottle. The whole procedure took a bit of getting used to, but once I mastered it, the process worked well to help Phillip get some milk into his tummy.

While we continued to help him work on his bottle skills, we settled in at a nearby housing facility for parents of child patients at UC San Francisco.

During this adoption adventure, I was still a full-time student at Idaho State, entrenched in mid-term exams and hefty research projects. But if all went well, I would be graduating the following month. I was excited about finally being done with school and having the freedom to concentrate on my new, larger family.

As our living situation had been thrown out of orbit all of a sudden, temporarily residing at the facility in San Francisco, I was having difficulty organizing a place and time to take exams and turn in papers for my classes. I contacted my instructors via email to let them know I was in a hospital-run residence awaiting the adoption of my new son, who was currently a patient at UCSF Medical Center, and I asked each professor to let me postpone the upcoming test or project. Two teachers replied with all-caps congratulatory wishes and said I could turn in my work a week late without any negative effect on my grade. Two other teachers responded that if they let me take a test/turn in a project late, they would have to let everyone take a test/turn in a project late. So, no. While the pressure was 50% off, I made an appointment to borrow the residence facility's computer to take a mid-term, conduct online research, and write a report. Thankfully, I was successful in each venture, completing all of the assignments and passing all the exams. I continued to study and do homework with books and notebook paper on the bed in our room between visits to see my redheaded boy.

After a couple days in San Francisco, we made plans to meet with Loretta and her son, Freddie, at a nearby park to allow our kids some play time, and to give us the opportunity to meet Phillip's biological brother. Walter and I had arranged to call Loretta at noon to discuss time and place.

When Walter dialed her number, Loretta answered the phone in tears. After a brief conversation, Walter hung up and immediately called the NICU front desk to request that Loretta be allowed in to visit Phillip.

Protocol required that plastic bracelets be given out to the mother and father of any NICU patient; one visitor at a time had to be accompanied by one bracelet-clad parent. In Phillip's situation, in the midst of an incomplete adoption, there were two sets of parents, adoptive and birth, and one set was being refused entrance.

With horror at my own insensitivity, I thought back on the moment before we first met Phillip.

While I had smiled with giddy excitement about the imminent introduction to my long-awaited new baby, the receptionist announced, "They can only go with the parents. Any visitor must be accompanied at all times by one of the parents with a bracelet. And we can only give out two bracelets.

Pauline tried to explain, "But these are the birth parents, and these are the adoptive parents."

Not budging from protocol, the attendant informed Pauline, "Well, the parents have to wear identification bracelets, and I can only give out two. And there can only be one guest per parent."

Pauline tried to tactfully explain the delicate situation; "The birth parents are going to want to visit and say goodbye and bring friends to say goodbye.

But there was no reasoning. The receptionist solved the problem her way, announcing, "Then they'll have to be guests of the adoptive parents and go in together. So, we'll have to take the bracelets off them [pointing at Loretta and Mike] and put new ones on the new parents."

In all the excitement, anticipation, explanation, and debate, the fact that Loretta's expression had been strained and her voice discontented didn't register in my mind at all. The problem still hadn't registered in my self-centered brain when the receptionist cut off Loretta's bracelet and, while putting on mine, said, "Congratulations!" to which Loretta rolled her eyes and snapped, "She hasn't even met him yet." I just looked at my new mommy's bracelet with pride, excited to get in and see my baby.

Now, Loretta was in hysterics. She had brought her best friend to come say good-bye to her baby boy, and had been refused entry to the NICU. The situation was already hard, but made worse by the fact that she, body still aching from the recent birth of a six-pound, 10-ounce baby, was not being given the freedom to bring conclusion to her situation in the way she emotionally required.

Walter explained the circumstances to the receptionist, and the next time Loretta went to the front desk, the attendant, without comment, handed over a third parent's bracelet. The worker's silence looked, to me, not like quiet acceptance, but embarrassment. I was glad that she felt ashamed, and hoped she'd learned to be more flexible and compassionate next time. I learned to be way more compassionate, too, and I was retroactively embarrassed by my self-centered, single-minded celebrating.

The NICU nurses were going through shift-change procedures and needed all visitors to remain in the lobby for 30 minutes. Walter and I sat with Loretta in a section of chairs near a small play area.

Heidi busied herself with some toy trains while Loretta opened up about some of the emotional turmoil she was going through.

"Everyone keeps saying he has Down syndrome. But he just looks like a normal baby. What is it? Sarah, what is it that makes them say he has Down syndrome?"

I thought for a moment. Of course, I wasn't qualified to make a real diagnosis, but I was able to list the physical features and attributes I had read about.

"Well, let me see. There's the eye shape…"

"But his eyes look fine. He looks like Freddie."

"There are also the palm creases…"

"But he doesn't have those."

"Yeah. Well, there's the newborn test they gave him—he got a little bit of a low score—seven out of 10."

"That's true. I don't know. I don't know what to think. They're doing the DNA test to make absolutely sure. Caden—Phillip—he has to stay in the NICU until he can drink from the bottle better, but what if they release him before the test results come in?"

"We would have to leave the housing facility. But we could stay in a hotel in San Francisco, if you want us to."

"I hate to make you guys stay so long, so far from home. I'm sure you have things to do."

"Well, we could go home, and if the test comes back negative, we could drive up here again."

"No, I wouldn't make you do that. We would come out to you and pick him up."

I understood what she meant, but I had a twinge of uneasiness. It felt like she meant they would come back and get him if he ended up being worthy of being raised. But wasn't he worthy now? He was just a little baby. Keeping in mind that I needed to be understanding of her experience and personal ordeal, I responded with a simple, "That's okay, we can decide that when the time comes."

"The hardest thing about all of this is," Loretta's eyes filled with tears, "Freddie has been so excited to be a big brother."

I thought, fleetingly, *He still is a big brother. He'll always be Phillip's big brother.*

Then I remembered the moment when Loretta handed Heidi her present—the shirt announcing, "I'm the Big Sister". I had even mentioned in our Dear Birth Parents letter that Heidi desperately wanted to become a big sister. Not only did Loretta collect up items to pass along to the new mommy, she actively went to the store to buy something for my daughter to celebrate her new status as big sister. Back at the hotel, I had heard Loretta mention, in passing, Freddie. Loretta was celebrating the event for my child when her heart was breaking for her own son. I hadn't thought once about how the situation that was causing my daughter such joy was breaking a little boy's heart.

And what about my own joy and Loretta's sorrow? In front of the hotel, when she handed over all those baby gifts to me, I just accepted them without a single thought about how this mother must have felt giving away her baby and everything that belonged to him. These gifts were presented to me by a mother who was probably going through the most traumatic experience of her life. Whatever her personal reasons, she was giving up her baby son but had taken the time to think of our joy—my joy as a mother—to gather up a bundle to present to me in congratulations.

Maybe I felt awkward, didn't know what to say, but did Loretta have any more of an advantage? The fact that she thought of my happiness during her despair should have touched my heart, but I was too focused on my own personal feelings of awkwardness at the meeting and excitement at the adventure. Watching Loretta, now crying in the NICU lobby, filled me with guilt. I knew I could do nothing to make her suffering any less acute, so I merely listened. But now, I actively listened with empathy.

"We told Freddie that the baby is sick and had to stay at the hospital. He's only two and a half, so we aren't going to mention the baby anymore. Then hopefully he'll forget."

I remembered the dreamlike memory I have of being in the hospital when I was two and a half with croup. Holding on to memories at such a young age is rare, but it's possible. I, like Loretta, hoped this wouldn't be the case for Freddie.

Chapter 14:

Goodbyes

On our sixth day in San Francisco, Phillip drank a two-ounce bottle in 35 minutes. He worked hard, and even though he didn't quite earn an A+ on his test, the charge nurse decided to go ahead and give him a passing grade.

Loretta gifted us with Freddie's old car seat. She hooked Phillip into the straps on her own and carried the seated child out to our car. I noted that Loretta looked like a natural holding that car seat—she'd held one less than two years before. I also noted, very clearly, that Loretta was trying to do as much for and with Phillip during their last few days together. I tucked that bit of information away into my mental baby book—someday I would tell Phillip that his birth mother did love him.

Hoping that the DNA test results would come in before we left town with Phillip, Loretta reserved a hotel room for us so we could stay in San Francisco for one more day. Mom flew back to Robinson Hills to prepare our house with clothes and diapers and to make other necessary preparations for our return.

In our hotel room, Heidi lay on a beige loveseat with her tiny baby brother in her arms. She held him tenderly and sang him a sweet, improvised lullaby while I took pictures and made a video, already the constantly-snapping-and-recording new mother. Then we, again, looked through the clothes from Loretta's big gift bag, deciding which outfits we liked most and wanted to dress Phillip in first.

We eventually realized that the sun was well set and hotel guests were no longer wandering the hallways. Walter and Heidi kissed Phillip's cheeks, bid me good-night, and went to the bed, but I remained wide-awake in the living section of our suite. I didn't want to waste time sleeping. Although Phillip was snoozing away, I spent most of the night staring at his handsome, unblemished, rosy face and feathery-soft ginger hair.

* * *

The next morning, having relinquished Phillip to Walter's care, I took a much-needed shower. While I was drying off and enjoying a sigh of cleanliness, I heard a female voice interspersed with the chirping sounds of more than one child, along with my husband's deeper tones. To avoid offending any innocent young visitors, I rapidly dressed before exiting the bedroom.

I discovered that the voices were coming from a friend of Loretta's, Yuki, who had come with her three young children to say good-bye to Phillip. Yuki held my baby, commented on his cuteness, let her daughter hold the tiny boy, and couldn't resist commenting, "How could anyone reject this beautiful being?"

That moment was the beginning of the most difficult day of the adoption experience in San Francisco. I soon found out that Yuki's sentiment was held by most of Loretta's friends and relatives.

We had made arrangements with Loretta to meet in the hotel lobby to let her friends come over and see Phillip one last time. When Walter and I, with Heidi holding Daddy's hand and Phillip in my arms, went out to the lobby, we soon found Loretta. She had a smileless face, appearing especially emotionally tense. From that point onward, the events of the next several hours blur in my memory.

Loretta's mother was there. When she saw me, she threw her arms around my neck and, her chest heaving with sobs, wailed, "She's going crazy! Why is she doing this? She's going crazy!" I didn't know what to do other than hug her back and repeat, "I'm sorry. I'm sorry." Betsy's baby grandson was being taken away, and she was helpless to stop it. She looked at me and begged, "He doesn't have Down syndrome. Those aren't Down syndrome features. He looks like everyone else in my family. He looks just like my son did when he was a baby. I told her I'd raise him, but she won't let me. Why is she doing this? She's going crazy!"

I heard an angry voice shout across the room. Turning my head, I saw Loretta throw up her hands and yell, "Mom!" followed by, "Dad, make her stop!" Shifting my uncomfortable gaze, I saw a tall, slim, gray-haired man wearing jeans and a white undershirt. Sternly, this man ordered, "Betsy!" and then motioned silently yet definitively for his wife to come toward him. Betsy immediately released her hold on my neck and scurried over to her husband. Trying not to stare, I peeked and saw Loretta's father, with a serious expression, quietly lecturing his wife.

After that instance, Betsy had no more public freak-outs, either at that location or anywhere else. However, for the next several hours in the hotel lobby, she spent every moment holding Phillip close, her face near his, talking and cooing, smiling and praising, only momentarily passing him to her husband to hold before taking him back into her own arms. She was visibly soaking in every ounce of grandmotherly bonding she possibly could during what she knew were her last moments with her grandson. I can only imagine that no amount of time could possibly have been enough.

Phillip seemed to know he was sharing a special last moment with his Grandma Betsy as well, or so I like to imagine. While Betsy held her grandson, his infant gaze suddenly focused sharply, and his eyes, for several seconds, widened and stared directly into the pupils of his loving grandmother. His stare was so fixed, so different from the weak, unstable eye movements that he had shown each waking moment since his birth, that Walter, Heidi, and I audibly gasped. I whipped out my camera to capture the moment when Phillip connected so deeply with his Grandma Betsy. There was a bond there that no separation could take away.

Hour after hour, we met friends and relatives, one after the next, all staying to take pictures, comment on Phillip's cuteness, and experience him before he left for good. Each person shook our hands and wished us well. Although I felt silently guilty for taking this baby away from their family, I was quite emotionally overcome by the generosity and graciousness of each person I met. A friend of Loretta's, knowing I had been absent for my own new son's baby shower, came to the hotel with a banner and decorations that had been used at the party, presenting them to me in a gift bag which was clipped shut with a clothespin that had been used for one of the games at the event. Betsy's best friend took me aside, wished us a safe drive home, shook my hand and left $60.00 in my palm. Loretta's brother visited the hotel after work to meet us and take a few pictures with his nephew. Everyone commented on Phillip's adorableness. I saw no more tears that day.

It seemed that nobody agreed with Loretta's decision. However, as I look back now, I understand that, really, nobody in her circle of family and friends was having the exact same experience as her. There could be opinions, but the only person who could see the situation through Loretta's eyes was Loretta.

Before she left the hotel lobby, Betsy and I exchanged contact information. During a later phone call, Betsy explained to Walter that, when Loretta's dad had been giving his quiet lecture, he told Betsy to knock off the crazy antics or else she was going to lose not only a grandson but a daughter, too. No matter how heartbreaking, decisions had been made, and Betsy needed to do what was necessary to keep the remaining family intact. So, from then on, whenever she was in the company of Loretta, she hid her unbearable grief.

Chapter 15:

Onward

The following morning, Walter and I, once again, went to the hotel lobby. This time, it was to meet with an adoption officer and sign some papers. With Heidi by my side and Phillip in my arms, after yesterday's highly-emotional series of events, the room seemed exceptionally quiet and peaceful.

While we were sitting with Joan, the officer, and autographing, I saw Loretta park her car and walk through the parking lot toward the hotel. I waved her over to our table.

She smiled and quietly requested, "I thought I could try feeding Phillip."

Phillip was still having a little difficulty with feedings, and I'm sure Loretta wanted to use that fact as an opportunity to spend a few moments with her baby before hotel check-out, when we would be going back home to Robinson Hills. I escorted Loretta to the hotel room, gave her a bottle, a burp cloth, and a redheaded child. Then I left her alone.

Back in the hotel lobby, Walter and I, Heidi playing on a nearby couch, sat with the adoption officer, signing and talking. Joan was a very intelligent older woman, gray and thin, with an intellectual's bespectacled face. Even though we have an open adoption, Joan had appeared surprised when she saw Loretta come into the lobby. I explained, "We have been seeing Loretta just about every day."

Curious, Joan asked, "Has Loretta told you what kind of arrangements she would like for visitation or correspondence with Phillip?"

I hadn't heard any mention of that concept from Loretta, Pauline, or anyone else. I told Joan so.

"Honestly," Joan admitted, "In these types of cases, even with an open adoption, the mother will often drop all contact with the baby. The emotional pain of giving birth to a disabled child is just too great."

I heard what she said, but didn't quite believe her. Loretta seemed to love Phillip. She was taking advantage of every possible moment to be with him. Why wouldn't she have a desire to keep in touch with and see Phillip for years to come? I told Joan, "Actually, I've been worrying about the opposite—that Loretta might change her mind and decide she wants to keep the baby."

"Well," Joan reminded us, "the parents do have the right to change their minds about the adoption within 30 days. However, it's been my experience that, in the case of special needs adoptions, the decision is pretty definite."

Joan went on, "When I signed the forms with Loretta, she talked about some of her personal concerns. One of her worries was that she wouldn't be able to emotionally handle the baby's heart surgery. So she wanted to know what would happen if you guys can't handle the heart surgery either. That's typical of what a parent in her situation might say—she can't emotionally handle it, so she doesn't want anyone else to be able to." I found that comment interesting and, free of judgment, made note of it in my mental journal.

Although I had only known Phillip for seven days, I was already starting to feel a mother's bond. Knowing that his birth mother, for the next month, had the right to take him back any time she wanted, made me try to resist the urge to fall in love with this tiny boy. Feeding a baby, tending to his needs, and watching his sleeping form all night made love difficult to fight. But, in order to avoid possible heartbreak, I tried to resist.

While Walter, Heidi and I packed our bags and checked out of the hotel room, Loretta continued holding Phillip. We even paid extra for late-checkout so birth mother and son could have a few more last moments together. With his feet against her tummy, his relaxed body lying on her legs, his shoulders on her knees, her hands under the back of his head, Loretta put her nose near Phillip's, looked into his eyes and softly cooed, "You're *very* cute." I've always remembered that sentence and the intonation she used. Although she didn't feel able to keep her baby, Loretta still was able to see Phillip's cuteness. I repeat the sentiment—"You're *very* cute"—to Phillip often, always in Loretta's honor.

When we were ready to start the journey back to southern California, Loretta, once again, put Phillip in his car seat. Carrying baby and seat out to the parking lot, Loretta stated firmly,

"I'm okay with this. I really am."

I wondered if she was trying to convince herself it was true, that she really was okay with what was about to happen. After so many moments of parental bonding over the last few days, and especially the last few hours, I don't think the concept of Loretta's regret was so much something I had to wonder about, but something I had to, sadly, view as unfortunately and undeniably true—she was trying to convince herself that the huge decision she had made was the right one, and that she could live with it.

Loretta secured Phillip's seat into the Corolla, gave us all hugs, and got into her own truck. Heidi sat to the right of Phillip's car seat, and I piled myself into the back seat on his left, "just in case" he needed me. We pulled out of the parking lot and followed Loretta's truck as she led us to the freeway entrance. When the onramp was in view, Loretta slowed and moved to the left, allowing us to pass. Our cars momentarily traveling adjacent to each other, we waved good-bye from our respective automobiles. She looked calm, matter-of-fact, business-like. Determinedly so. She didn't smile.

We never saw her again.

Chapter 16:

Home

We took our time driving home, stopping often for leg stretches, food, potty breaks, diaper changes, and even a little bit of sight-seeing. Stopping at a dried fruit and nut stand, I walked around flats of bagged and arranged raisins and cashews, carrying Phillip, looking at goods to buy but not intending to purchase, my only goal to show off the tiny redhead in my arms. I was already a proud mom.

Loretta had asked me to call her when we got home safely, but our trip was taking a bit longer than expected. At 10:00 PM, before they went to bed, I called Loretta's cell phone—Mike answered. I asked if Loretta was there, and he said she wasn't able to come to the phone. I let him know that we were all fine, and I noted, mentally, that this might be the clean break from her special-needs child that the adoption specialist had spoken of. Or perhaps Loretta was too emotional to talk on the phone. Either way, I felt sorry for her situation—and a bit guilty.

Our return to Robinson Hills wasn't exactly smooth. After the long drive from San Francisco, at 11:30 PM, red-eyed and yawning, Walter, Heidi and I walked into the house, hauling baby-gear, baby-gifts, and an actual baby, to find that our dog, left in the care of a friend, had pooped all over the couch. So, before plopping down in an exhausted heap on the sofa to cuddle our new child, we had to scrape off actual plop, then shampoo and disinfect. It wasn't the welcome homecoming we were looking toward. Still, it was our reality. We were glad to be in town with helpful relatives and friends nearby.

I had to recommence studying the very next day, as graduation was coming up in mere weeks. Luckily, Phillip was tiny and sleepy, and when he was awake he didn't go far. I often laid him across my lap with his head resting on the crook of my elbow while I typed away on my laptop or read and highlighted textbooks.

Although our home study was completed and Phillip was in our arms, the adoption was far from finished. We still had to wait 28 more days while Loretta was allowed to change her mind about relinquishment and have Phillip immediately returned to her. We had been assured, repeatedly, that Loretta would not be changing her mind; still, I wouldn't feel completely at ease until that 30 days period, since he was discharged from the hospital and placed into our care, had elapsed.

Pauline had told me two horrifying stories of birth mothers taking their children back. One newborn child was taken back within the 30-day period, heartbreakingly for the adoptive mother, but she soon began the adoption process a second time, now with a little two-year-old boy. At 11:50 PM of the 30th day, police officers came to the adoptive mother's house to take the toddler from his bed and hand him back to his birth mom. Worst of all, both situations had happened to the same adoptive mother. Pauline's story ended happily enough with the adoptive mother finally successfully keeping a third child to call her own, but that didn't make me any less nervous about the possibilities of my own adoptive situation.

My mother and I were both fearful of becoming too attached to tiny Phillip within that long month, but our little boy made resisting love impossible. When Phillip was about two weeks old, Mom was cradling him in the living room rocking chair. As Phillip began to peacefully doze, I noticed that Mom was crying.

Before I could ask her what was wrong, she admitted, "I'm worrying about losing him."

That would have been a nightmare, having Phillip taken back from not only us but his new grandparents as well. I understood, clearly, my mom's worry.

I did my best to keep my feelings for Phillip like that of a teacher or neighbor—I was just spending time with him, but he wasn't mine. Often, as I held him and gazed into his big blue eyes, I found the words, "I love you," forming on my lips. But I would always stop myself immediately after the "I" escaped. In my heart, though, I couldn't deny the truth. I loved him the minute I saw his eyes in his little NICU isolet. He was the child I had been waiting for. Losing him at this point would have destroyed me.

During one of our chats with Betsy, she told us that Loretta called her and said, "Yeah, the DNA test just came back and confirmed Down syndrome." Betsy told us, "She definitely won't want him back now. You have nothing to worry about." That ended up being true.

After weeks of worry, thirty of the longest days in my entire life finally passed. With great relief, on July 22, Phillip was staying without danger of being taken back by his birth family. To celebrate, my sign language interpreter friends threw us a baby shower to welcome Phillip into our home. Dena offered her house for the celebration; she provided guests with tiny onesies and permanent markers to decorate and personalize little outfits for my new son. Most of all, everyone enjoyed loving and experiencing the perfect presence of Phillip. Denise held and fawned over Phillip for hours—I finally convinced her she had to let other people have a turn. Naomi bonded with Phillip and became his Soul Sister—they both share the experience of having been adopted. Amber looked like a natural mom holding a baby in her arms. And Billie continued to make note that Phillip looked an awful lot like Beaker. My friends welcomed Phillip into their lives willingly, openly, and lovingly, just like I had given birth to him myself. I showed him off and passed him around like a proud mom should, and I told him repeatedly that I loved him. The sense of relief after those nerve-racking 30 days was huge.

During the previous month's wait, Phillip had been my scholastic good luck charm: he helped me pass all of my classes. When graduation time came, the first time I ever set foot on the ISU campus, it was decided that Phillip's heart was too weak to withstand the stress of airplane flight. So Walter and I, Heidi, my dad, and my step-mom, went up to Pocatello, Idaho while Phillip stayed back in Robinson Hills with Mom and Rob. But I brought with me an 8"x10" framed picture of Phillip and held it when I walked up to receive my diploma.

He couldn't be with me in person, but he was still in my arms. He was finally there, and I wasn't letting go.

Chapter 17:

Family

Phillip's relationships with his grandparents are exactly what I thought each of them would be. My mom loves her Phillip deeply and often looks at him and tells me, "I'm so glad you ended up with a little boy. He has brightened our lives." The closeness of their bond is unsurprising.

Minnie adores her grandson—to her, J.J. When we visit her condo, little J.J. runs down the hall to be swooped up by his GrandMinnie, and he has spent many hours snuggling in her lap. After those worrying questions and comments when we first told her of our plan to adopt, Minnie has never said a negative word about him, instead only praising him for his universal skill and intelligence, as I knew she would. Now that the mystery of Down syndrome has been removed for her, she can relax in the joy of her amazing new grandson. She's immensely proud.

Dad is generally reserved, but not when it comes to showing affection for his namesake. He has no problem holding Phillip to partake in a bit of singing, reading, knee-bouncing, or just plain cuddling. I remember one time when Phillip threw his arms out for a hug, and my dad couldn't help but blurt an animated, almost involuntary, "I love you!" Moments like that are especially rewarding for me. They make me certain that my determination to adopt was the right thing to do.

After bonding with my son for many months, Dad admitted to me, "When you told me you were adopting a baby with Down syndrome, I thought to myself, 'What is this thing she's doing?' I was worried. I didn't want you to get hurt. But now that we have him, I understand. He's just like other kids."

Danny, my father in law, had a reaction that continues to puzzle us. Shortly after Phillip came into our home, Danny visited us. He spent several minutes talking to and horsing around with Heidi, but when I said, "Do you want to hold the baby?" he replied curtly and definitively, "No. No." To this day, he has never held his grandson.

Even more confusing, he has never again participated in another Special Olympics.

Danny's lack of interest in Phillip left me confused, but Walter reminded me—when the school labeled Walter's older brother as dyslexic, Danny responded by saying, "That's not possible. There's no way I can have a disabled son." Walter is of the opinion that Danny can also not have a disabled grandson. We've decided, jointly, not to worry about his reasons and leave him in peace. Danny hasn't contacted us in years.

Since bringing Phillip from San Francisco to Robinson Hills, Walter and I, and even my mom, have spent many tearful hours on the telephone with Betsy. Losing a grandchild was a terrible tragedy for Betsy, and we have kept that fact in mind as much as possible; we do whatever possible to allow Betsy the access to Phillip and our family that she needs to grieve and heal. To Phillip and Heidi both, Betsy is Grandma Betsy. She sends each child a Christmas and birthday gift every year, and has even sent hand-me-down clothes to Heidi from one of Phillip's biological cousins. Keeping in touch has been important for Betsy but, as we are well aware, has not been a sufficient replacement for knowing her grandson personally and watching him grow.

Since the last day at the hotel in San Francisco, save for one emailed request for photos when Phillip was one month old, we have never heard from Loretta.

We didn't know a lot about the situations surrounding Loretta's decision to put Phillip up for adoption, but through the months after arriving home with Phillip, Betsy has gradually told us the whole story.

When Loretta was giving birth, the delivery came very quickly. She couldn't stop pushing, so her baby was ejected out too rapidly, causing the bridge of his nose to swell up a bit. But after he was born and cleaned up, the nurse brought Caden to his mother for his first breastfeeding.

Loretta took the baby in her arms, looked at him, and said, "He looks like something's wrong. I don't want to feed him."

Betsy assured her, "He's fine. His little nose is swollen from the birth, but other than that he's just a normal baby."

"I don't want to feed him," Loretta insisted. "Something's telling me not to bond with him." She refused to nurse, and he was given bottled formula.

The next morning, Betsy again came to the hospital to visit daughter and grandson. She was walking toward Loretta's room when she heard screams erupt from down the hallway. It was Loretta's voice. Betsy broke into a run and burst into the room. Her daughter was howling and crying, "No! No!" A nurse was there as well, who explained to Betsy, "The baby has been identified as having Down syndrome."

Then, Mike walked in with Freddie. By this time, Betsy was crying as well, and seeing his mommy and grandmother in tears, Freddie started to weep. Betsy took Freddie in her arms while Mike tried to comfort Loretta. Soon, Freddie was removed from the hospital to save him additional trauma, and Caden was transferred to UC San Francisco to begin testing and treatments. The brothers have never been in the same room together since.

Listening quietly to the story being related to me by Betsy, I was flooded by confusing, conflicting emotions. When the traumatic event in Loretta's hospital room took place, I didn't even know of the baby's existence. However, during the relating of the story, my maternal urge to protect my baby was in full force. I had an overwhelming grief at not having properly protected my baby during those tumultuous moments in Loretta's hospital room. With so much screaming and bawling, I longed to jump into Doctor Who's TARDIS, go back to be present at that moment, and save my boy. I wanted to sweep him into my arms and tell him how loved he was. He was so tiny, so innocent, and so deserving of the overwhelming joy and unconditional love of a new mother. I longed to give him what he deserved.

Betsy had offered, repeatedly, to raise Caden herself, but Loretta flatly and repeatedly refused. When Betsy wanted to know why, Loretta simply insisted that her decision had been made and she would not budge. After prodding, Loretta finally admitted, "I'm afraid of losing my husband." Betsy told us she wasn't sure what that comment meant and she didn't pry.

I didn't get to know Mike well at all. I hardly saw him, and when I did, he didn't talk too much. Therefore, anything I might think about why he did or didn't want Phillip would only be speculation. And Loretta had her personal reasons for preferring to give up her baby than lose her husband. My personal opinion is, however, that if I had to choose between keeping Walter or Heidi, Walt could take a hike.

After telling Freddie the baby had to be left at the hospital, Caden was never again spoken of in Freddie's presence. However, from that experience in the hospital onward, Freddie was obsessed with babies. He looked at babies, commented on them, talked to them, wanted to hold them. Loretta's belief that Freddie would forget was unrealized.

An event as traumatic as the one Freddie experienced in the hospital, watching all of his closest family members crying, could never be forgotten. When Freddie was three years old, his little friend at school came in talking about his new baby brother, and Freddie immediately chimed in, "I have a baby brother, too."

I don't know what prompted me to tell my very empathetic, very sensitive daughter about the conversation, but I related to her the story of what Betsy told me happened with Freddie.

"You mean," Heidi asked, "Phillip's big brother doesn't know he has a baby brother?"

I explained, "Well, Loretta thought it would be best if they let Freddie forget. He seems to have some memory of a baby brother, but they thought it would hurt Freddie less if they tried to help him forget."

Heidi's eyes began to glisten. "But he needs to know he has a baby brother. Phillip is going to grow up, and then he won't be a baby anymore. Then Freddie will never get to see Phillip when he was a baby."

Heidi began to cry a pure, heartfelt, innocent despair from a child who was being informed of an unfairness like she never believed possible. Her heart broke for Freddie.

"You have to call Freddie and tell him he has a baby brother! You have to tell him before Phillip isn't a baby anymore!" She sobbed, "Please, Mom, promise me you'll tell him! He has to know before it's too late! Oh, *God*!"

My beautiful daughter, so in love with her baby brother, was heartbroken that his babyhood was being withheld from another innocent sibling. That fact, to Heidi, was an injustice that she could not emotionally bear.

Of course, I explained to Heidi, I did not have the right to be the one who lets Freddie know about Phillip. But that fact did nothing to quell her grief. She curled up on the couch and cried for a long time.

As Phillip's mom, I do have very strong feelings on the subject. In the future, when Freddie finally finds out he has a younger brother, I firmly predict there is going to be anger and regret over lies and years lost.

* * *

In our country's recent past, doctors would almost always recommend that parents institutionalize their babies with Down syndrome. In fact, when I was showing Phillip off to an old friend from my high school, the friend informed me that he had a sister with Down syndrome living in an institution in New York, all the way across the country from the Robinson Hills home where he grew up. I knew his whole family, but none of them had ever mentioned the fact that they had an additional sibling. Institutionalization was a standard medical-professional's suggestion, and many families took the doctor's advice.

In the new millennium, doctors will often offer abortion as one of the first options when a baby with Down syndrome is identified. My cousin's unborn baby was identified as having Down syndrome, and medical professionals suggested to her no less than three times that she should consider abortion. At first, the doctor didn't suggest abortion but rather assumed it. "Your baby has Down syndrome, so we need to schedule the termination." I am so blessed that she chose to tell her doctor that termination was not an option and raised her baby girl. Now first cousins can experience Down syndrome together.

Another one of my friends was pregnant with a baby that tested positive for Down syndrome. Her doctor actually informed her of the diagnosis by saying, "Your baby has Down syndrome. I suggest you do the world a favor and don't bring another disabled child into it. In fact, if you have time, we can take care of it right now." Luckily, my friend told the doctor to step aside so she could leave his office and never come back. She has since given birth to the blondest, most beautiful girl—who also has Down syndrome—I've ever seen.

Today, although many mothers still abort these gorgeous babies, the ones that are born are either snatched up by parents on lists hundreds long waiting to adopt them, or they are successfully and joyfully raised by their biological parents. The quality of life for people with Down syndrome has improved rapidly and exponentially, and by the time Phillip is 18, society will have evolved even farther— Freddie will have met at least one or two people with Down syndrome, or other syndromes, and wonder why he was kept from the one that is related to him.

I cannot predict the future with absolute certainty, of course, but I've kept a detailed library of photographs and videos of Phillip just in case Freddie wants to see those records someday. If Freddie can't be with Phillip now, I will let him, when the time comes, see what his brother was like from beginning to present.

Chapter 18:

Care

About three weeks after we brought Phillip to Robinson Hills, I got a call at home from a woman who introduced herself as Linda.

"I heard that you've adopted a baby boy. Congratulations!"

I wondered how she knew, but I didn't mind her call, so I didn't ask. Her voice was chipper and friendly, and I looked forward to talking to someone who was congratulating me about my son.

"Because your baby has Down syndrome, he is eligible for services from the Pine Valley Regional Center for any therapies he might need. I'd like to come by to see Phillip and evaluate him."

We looked at our individual calendars and made an appointment. Linda came by our house the following week to go ooh and aah over Phillip, ask Walter and me some questions, evaluate Phillip for service needs, and show us pictures of her own son, also with Down syndrome.

Thus began our relationship with PVRC, Linda, and numerous therapists. Paid for by the state, Phillip started getting weekly home visits from an occupational therapist, a physical therapist, and a speech therapist. When he was a little older, he also began a weekly play group with other disabled children and their parents where they could join together and sing songs or play in a therapeutic recreation area with sensory and motor assistive equipment. The services we received were indescribably beneficial, informative, and even fun.

When Phillip started walking, his physical therapist, Ruth, began meeting with him at a local park so she could work with him to improve walking abilities on various surfaces like grass or sand, as well as climbing up steps and going down a slide. His occupational therapist, Brigitte, taught Phillip the joys of keys, balls, and Cheerios, while also surreptitiously teaching him how to use his hands and fingers effectively for future self-care skills. Every several months, Linda and the therapists would meet with Walter and me, Mom and Papa, to discuss Phillip's previous and new goals, and to ask us what we'd like to see him accomplish in the upcoming months. I'd mention anything I'd like to see Phillip learn to do, such as smile or babble or sing a song, and Linda would translate any of those desires into some age-appropriate future goals for him and the therapists to begin working on.

I felt so grateful for all the work and care from Linda and the regional center. Linda became a resource to answer any questions or concerns, including when my cousin's baby was refused services by her local regional center. When I emailed Linda on my cousin's behalf, she immediately called back and ranted, "State services are automatically provided for children with Down syndrome. Your cousin's baby can't be refused services. If you need me to call anyone, let me know and I will." I'm proud to say that this beautiful woman who cares so deeply has also become a friend.

Down syndrome not only gave us a wonderful son, but it made us members of a new community of people who appreciate and love their family members with Down syndrome as much as I do. I feel honored to be accepted as a new member of this society.

When we found Phillip, I decided to quit my job at the college. Since he would be needing heart surgery, I wanted a more flexible work schedule so that I could shift my calendar as necessary and take adequate time off. I started working as a freelance sign language interpreter, taking various interpreting assignments in the community.

At our old house in El Segundo, Walter and I had enrolled Heidi into a childcare establishment, Kendra's Caring Days, when she was three months old. We were lucky to find that absolutely stellar childcare facility near the college where we could feel completely comfortable leaving our daughter every day. But our current house was an hour away, one way, from Kendra's, and I was no longer working at the college. So, although we did momentarily consider the option, we knew that Caring Days was not a logical placement for Phillip.

Mom and Rob had generously agreed to care for Phillip while I worked, but I did worry for their wellbeing—although both active and healthy, their child raising days were long-since passed, and I didn't want them to wear themselves out raising grandchildren. We unanimously decided to search locally for daycare options for Phillip.

Mom, ever resourceful, obtained a list of local childcare centers. She contacted Linda and was supplied with 20 or so names, addresses, and phone numbers of licensed childcare facilities in Robinson Hills. I went back to work, and Mom began making calls.

One by one, Mom found childcare options full, not looking for new children. Several owners gave us the names and numbers of additional recommended centers, but most were already on the list and already impacted. After a plethora of calls, Mom did find one center open. We made an appointment, I took time off work, and we went for an interview.

Mom and I brought Phillip to meet a husband and wife who ran a small childcare out of their home. They had a large add-on room which expanded the available care-area of the living room by double. The home was fully equipped for the entertainment and care of their little charges. Out of the add-on's large windows, the spacious back yard and swing set were welcomingly viewable. Their house was clean, the owners inviting and friendly.

Very importantly, the couple seemed to like Phillip and the idea of caring for him. They talked to him and held him and squealed with joy when he smiled. I felt lucky to have found them.

Then, the wife asked the tone-changing question:

"Would it be alright with you if we teach him about Jesus Christ?"

My heart instantly sank. Walter is culturally Jewish, but was not raised going to temple or celebrating the traditional holy days, although his mother did decorate a tree and fill stockings every Christmas. Heidi self-identifies as Jewish, requesting that we celebrate Hanukkah on her behalf, which we do ineptly yet gladly. And I, although raised Catholic, am now decidedly secular.

To get out of the immediate impending awkwardness, I smiled and replied with my standard half-truth, "We're Jewish."

"Oh, no problem at all," said the wife. "I'm glad we asked!" We all laughed and grinned politely.

After cheerfully wrapping up the meeting, Mom and I took our leave.

As soon as we were outside, crossing the lawn to our car, I said dejectedly, "Oh well, so much for that."

"Maybe you should think about it," Mom suggested, "before you make a decision. They were so good with Phillip."

That was a really important point. My boy's safety and happiness were vital, and he would have the security of both with this couple, I felt certain. I mentally debated the issue a few minutes longer before I finally said, "I'll wait and talk it over with Walter and see what he wants to do." I couldn't make such a big decision on my own.

The decision didn't take long to make. When I told Walter about the couple, he decided for me.

"If their religion is that strong that they're going to be teaching the kids about it, then it will come up eventually, no matter what we tell them our preferences are. Phillip will be there when they're teaching other kids about Jesus. So, no, I'm not comfortable with that."

In the end, we decided to keep looking for childcare, and if we couldn't find anyone else, we'd go back to the Christian couple. Anyway, Phillip would only be in their care until he was three, and then he would begin early-start preschool for disabled children. But in the meantime, I called the very nice couple and let them know we liked them a lot, but we had a change of plans and we would contact them again in the future if need for their care resurfaced.

Searching for childcare recommenced.

While I went on daily community interpreting assignments, Mom continued making unsuccessful call after unsuccessful call. Finally, she found another available daycare provider, this one, very close to our home in another private residence. We made an appointment for a visit.

Upon entering the one-story neighborhood tract home, Mom and I were very pleased by what we saw. Our knock at the bright white front door was answered by the lady of the house, a young woman, comfortably yet neatly dressed, long dark hair pulled away from her charming face in a modest clip at the back of her neck.

She smiled and politely asked, "Sarah?"

"Yes!" I responded with a grin and a handshake. "It's very nice to meet you. This is my mom, Alex."

"Very nice to meet you. I am Sanjana."

"And this is Phillip." I indicated my pride and joy, awake, quietly enjoying a relaxing recline in my arms.

"Please, come in." she said formally yet sweetly. She stepped aside to welcome us into her abode.

And gosh, what an abode! From the entryway, every visible room was tastefully furnished and sparsely decorated, the way I always wished my own home was—comfortably non-distracting to the eye, and ultimately child-proof. Even with three small children playing in the living room, the carpet was white without so much as a dime-sized spot anywhere. There, seated on a clean beige loveseat with a baby already in her arms, was another woman, a little older, but just as fit and healthy as the woman who was now guiding us to sit on the couch.

"This is my mother-in-law. She works with me every day."

We shook hands all around. Then it was time to show Phillip off.

Sanjana took Phillip into her arms, where he lay comfortably, looking curiously into her eyes. But when Sanjana passed my boy to her mother-in-law, the baby she was holding now peacefully crawling at her feet, Phillip started smiling and cooing almost instantly. The three of us laughed and commented on Phillip's obvious preference for grandmothers. The two of them really seemed to bond, and I imagined a great connection in the future for this pair.

We told Sanjana that we would like childcare on Mondays and Tuesdays. Part time care, she responded, was no problem at all. Phillip would have physical therapy on Tuesdays, and the therapist would need to come to Sanjana's house for an hour on those days. A therapist, Sanjana assured us, would be welcome in their home. Everything went smoothly, and I was able to breathe a sigh of relief—we had found our childcare.

"Then," Sanjana concluded, "we will see you at 7:00 AM on Monday."

"Oh, thank you so much," I gushed. "This is such a relief for all of us."

I retrieved Phillip and we waved goodbye. Bundled back into the car, Phillip fell quickly asleep, so that when we returned to Mom's house, I gingerly removed him from his car seat harness and lay him directly in bed. I used the opportunity of babylessness to partake in a little celebratory nap of my own.

In an hour, I woke up and stumbled into the living room to hear my mom's disappointed voice say, "I have bad news."

"What?" After such a productive and lucky day, I had no idea what could be bad news.

"Sanjana called right after we got home. They've decided they don't want to accept Phillip."

"Why? She said we could start on Monday. Why won't they accept him now?"

Mom explained, "She told me, 'All the other children here are healthy.'"

I was shocked. After months of people going gaga over my baby, telling me how adorable he is, praising his cuteness and red hair, he was now being completely rejected simply due to who he is. I was angry, dumbfounded, hurt. But most of all, I was motivated. Thanks to Dad for teaching me the power of motivation. The Americans with Disabilities Act ensures that all people, such as innocent babies, can't be discriminated against on the basis of disability. Sanjana wasn't going to do that to any more kids.

I made a rapid dash to my mom's computer and began researching the law as it relates to in-home childcare. The proof I needed wasn't hard to find. In minutes, I located the U.S. Department of Justice's website and the section that relates to the ADA, Title III: Public Accommodations.

With cyber evidence at hand, I went about composing one of my long letters. In this composition, I described the reasons why Sanjana's rejection of Phillip was so very, very wrong.

Dear Sanjana,

My family enjoyed meeting you recently, and we were very much looking forward to following through with our mutual decision to begin child care services at your residential day care center. We were saddened to receive the message that, due to the fact that he is disabled, you decided against having our son, Phillip, participate in your child care.

We would like to make it clear that this letter is not written in order to persuade you to allow our son to participate in your day care center. However, for your education, we would like to inform you of a few points regarding your decision.

First of all, exclusion of our son from your day care is a direct violation of the law. According to the Americans with Disabilities Act (ADA), a child cannot be excluded from day care, even small family-owned day-care centers, due to the fact that the child in question has a disability. Caregivers may not use unfounded preconceptions or stereotypes to make decisions about excluding disabled children from their child-care centers. With this letter, we have included some literature about the ADA; we suggest that you read this literature so that you can avoid complications with the ADA and any future disabled children who are introduced to your child-care service.

Regarding these future potential clients, we would like to make sure you are aware of the impact that your decision could have on your business. As parents who are currently actively networking to obtain day-care services, it is likely that your practice of excluding disabled children might be mentioned, not only to service providers but to other parents. A small business that is trying to obtain new clients ought to be careful about making the decision to show blatant discrimination against children.

On the subject of children, we would like to make sure you are aware of the impact that your decision had on our family. Imagine how you might feel if someone told you that they did not want your lovely son in their home, simply because of the person that he is. This is what you did to us, and your prejudice against our tiny baby has caused us great sadness. However, your action has also taught us that, even at a mere five months old, we already have to learn to fight for the rights of our marvelous son; for that, we are grateful.

Thank you for taking the time to read this letter and learn about the laws which pertain to our amazing son, Phillip. We hope that your future business decisions can be more successful.

Sincerely,
Walter and Sarah Cavilry

I sent off my fully packed envelope and never heard a reply. So be it—I was simply glad to have taught her something about business and gotten the last word. My search for childcare continued.

Mom had one more name on her list of potential childcare providers. This one, yet another private home, was just down the street from my dad's house, not as handy for Mom, but still in a convenient-enough location.

Walter and I made an appointment with LaRue, the owner of this center. When LaRue opened her door, she greeted us with a weak smile, appearing very relaxed, almost sleepy. She was dressed in shorts and a spaghetti-strapped tank top, her curly blonde hair surrounding her face and shoulders like an unwieldy flaxen riot.

The house was clean and tidy—there were several toys available for the kids to effortlessly access. The place looked fine. LaRue led us through the house and to her kitchen. We put Phillip, in his car seat carrier, up on the kitchen table. The three adults sat on stools surrounding Phillip's perch.

We exchanged polite conversation, and LaRue spoke quietly to Phillip. Nothing was going particularly wrong, but I felt awkward. LaRue seemed—not quite right. Had she just woken up? Was she merely very laid-back? I just couldn't figure her out. It seemed to me that I had to prompt her to give us all the information we needed. What were her facility's hours of operation? Would she accept part-time attendance? How much was the monthly charge?

After some time, we got all the general questions answered. Then we brought up the idea of having Phillip's occupational therapist come by for the weekly sessions. LaRue (lethargically) welcomed the idea of having the therapist in her home once a week—no problem.

With that, and not quite knowing what else to talk about, it seemed like all bases were covered and we said our goodbyes, confirming that we would be back to start weekly care the following Monday.

In the car, Walter let me know how he was really feeling about LaRue.

"I'm not happy."

"I know. Neither am I," I agreed. "But we can't find anyone else. And I'm worried about Mom. She has Phillip all day every day and can't play bridge with her friends or run errands. And she must be tired."

"Yeah, but I'm horrified by the idea of leaving Phillip with that lady."

"I'm not so thrilled about it, but what else can we do? What about the Christians?"

Walter admitted, "I'm not thrilled about that either."

"Well, maybe it's just her personality. She might be fine. We could just try LaRue for a few weeks and see how it goes. Mom has called everyone on the list. I just don't see what else we can do at this point."

With that, we agreed to follow through and bring Phillip to LaRue the following week.

For two weeks, Walter brought Phillip to LaRue on Monday and Tuesday and I picked him up in the afternoon. Each time I arrived, she was sitting with Phillip in an overstuffed chair, holding him on her lap. She would never get up, greet me, or make any movement to hand Phillip over to my care. She would just give me a Mona Lisa smile and keep sitting, never telling me about the day, what my son had eaten, how he had slept—nothing. Not the warm, fuzzy type, a complete 180 degree difference from Kendra's traditionally exuberant and welcoming, "How was *your* day?" Being in LaRue's presence always made me feel weird.

Mom organized with all involved to have an occupational therapy session at 2:00 PM at the childcare center on Tuesday of Phillip's third week with LaRue. Phillip had already been dropped off at LaRue's house that morning. The plan was that Brigitte, the current occupational therapist, would arrive at the care center at 2:00. My mom arranged to be present as well so that she could learn any new exercises for further reinforcement back at her home.

At 2:00 sharp, Brigitte, my mom at her side, rang LaRue's doorbell.

No answer.

The two of them waited a few minutes, giving each other confused looks, before ringing again.

After another long pause, the door slowly opened.

There stood LaRue, looking particularly nonplussed. Her hair was rumpled and her eyes red, giving the distinct appearance of someone who had recently pried herself out of bed.

With a look of condemnation, she growled, "Your *appointment* was for *three*." She let them come inside and proceeded to roll her eyes and frown for the remainder of their visit.

A misunderstanding in regard to timing? Understandable. But her cranky response to my son's therapist and grandmother was exceedingly unprofessional. I especially didn't like finding out that my mother had been spoken to with such disrespect. Not cool.

And speaking of uncool, where was my infant son while LaRue, obviously, napped? Perhaps Phillip had been left in the care of LaRue's teenage daughter. The young lady might have been perfectly ethical and responsible, but even if she was, I had never talked to her or entrusted my son to her care. And I wasn't even sure Phillip had been left with any adult at all while LaRue was snoozing. Learning of the new air of unprofessionalism, I wasn't about to cut her any slack.

As the rest of Mom's story goes, she and Brigitte, quietly and awkwardly, worked with Phillip through his 45-minute therapy exercises and left. At 4:00, having already been called by my mom to be made aware of the 2:00 events, I picked Phillip up and brought him home.

The following day, Walter visited LaRue and picked up a refund check for the remainder of that month's prepaid tuition. She handed the funds over without question, sneering silently.

As a consequence of those events and our previous difficulties in finding ideal daycare services, Mom and Rob rearranged their personal calendars and announced to us that they would care for Phillip until he started preschool.

I still think back on the Christian couple. I rejected them and chose LaRue? That's embarrassing—not my proudest mommy decision. If I had just sucked it up and utilized their services, I could have given Mom and Rob a break every week.

But I'm sure thankful, every day, for all my mom and stepdad have done to help Phillip and our family. I don't know how we would get by without them.

And every time we pass the area of LaRue's house, Walter says with a shiver, "I'm so glad we got Phillip out of there."

Chapter 19:

Rob

As Betsy told me, she and Loretta rarely talked to each other about the adoption. One scolding in the hotel lobby was enough for Betsy, and she kept the peace by keeping silent. But on one rare instance, a tearful daughter posed a question, disguised as a statement, to her mother.

"You hate me."

Betsy, shocked, begged, "What do you mean?"

Loretta explained, "You hate me for giving away Caden."

Mother and daughter tearfully hugged for a long time. "I don't hate you," Betsy consoled Loretta. "I will always love you. The decision you made was very hard. God used you as a vessel to bring a family the little baby they have always wanted."

Loretta sighed, "I hope that's true."

"Now," Betsy went on, "maybe God will prove that's true by giving you the baby girl you were hoping for."

Betsy paused in her story to admit to us, "Why did I say that to her? I wanted her to feel better, but now if she doesn't have a girl, Loretta will think God is telling her she made the wrong decision with Caden."

Thankfully, Betsy's prediction came true. One and a half years after Phillip's birth, Loretta delivered a healthy little girl. The new baby, named Harmony, had some minor orthopedic issues, but she overcame those obstacles and grew into a healthy, raven-haired toddler.

In the following months, we began to hear less from Betsy. We could have chosen to be concerned or offended by the distancing, but the reasons for her absence were logical. During one heartbreakingly candid phone call, Betsy, through sobs, admitted the reason why she hadn't sent her traditional Christmas gifts for Phillip and Heidi the previous December.

Firstly, Betsy explained that her husband's business was far from booming. Expenses were high, income was low, and bills were going unpaid. In fact, they were in real danger of losing their house. Letters and calls to a far-away, long-unseen child were, of course, farther down the list than saving their means of shelter and food.

Additionally, Loretta would often leave Freddie with Betsy during the day, sometimes for the whole weekend. Now with a granddaughter to care for as well while Loretta and Mike worked, Grandma Betsy's schedule was often full with babysitting duties. This, as an unexpected after effect, had caused some additional strife between mother and daughter, as Freddie and Harmony seemed to enjoy being with their grandmother more than they liked being with Mommy. Through tears, Betsy told me that the stressors of house and family together were dreadfully depressing.

Lastly, although it wasn't verbalized, I'm sure time had softened the pain of loss. When my baby twins died, I cried constantly and thought of them, literally, every waking moment for weeks. Over time, of course, I thought of them less and less. Now, 10 years later, although I never remove my double-hearted pendent necklace, those two little angels come to my mind only occasionally. I'm sure, although not identical, the situation for Betsy must be similar. I have absolutely no doubt in my mind that Grandma Betsy still loves her grandson, but Phillip's absence for these years must have lessened the grief. I hold nothing against her for that; I only hope, for the sake of her grandmotherly loving heart, it's true.

Luckily, Phillip has not been lacking in grandparents. When Phillip appeared in our lives, the initial reservations of all grandparents completely disappeared. Three quarters of a mile from my home is the street where I grew up, and where my mother lives with Rob. My daughter calls my mom "Grammy," and we planned to teach Phillip that title as well.

Rob, however, had never exhibited a close bond with any of the Cavilrys. He had always been rather reserved and quiet, rarely talking, and absolutely never laughing—only occasionally smiling. I often felt like an unwanted presence in their home, as if he might have preferred complete silence to the disruptive sound of my mother and me watching a movie and giggling together. He was, and still is, a good man—a very good man—who cares deeply about the environment, wildlife, conservation, and the preservation of our planet. However, in the wet-noodle department, he seemed to be an expert. The two of us didn't have a close relationship and, although I respected him as my mom's husband, we never had much in common.

Then came Phillip.

I was grateful that, when I finished my maternity leave and went back to work, my mom offered to baby-sit during the day. At three months old, Phillip was pretty easy to care for—just diapers, feeding, and holding. Still, I made sure to hurry and collect my baby at the end of every work day, as I didn't want his presence to disturb the peace of Rob's quiet domicile.

One evening after work, I had several pressing, time-constrained errands to run. I hurried to Mom's house, gathered up my son, put him in his car seat, and looked over my shoulder to pull out of the driveway when I saw Rob come out of the front door. I rolled down the passenger-side window; Rob leaned in and said,

"You can leave Phillip here until you're done. He's really no trouble."

I was very grateful; errands would be much easier to run sans infant.

But I was a little taken aback. My mother had actually just left the house to take care of some errands of her own, meaning Rob had no choice but to be completely disrupted by Phillip's presence—he would actually be caring for the baby by himself. But now, Rob was volunteering to take charge of the boy for what would be about 3 hours. Reservations aside, I went ahead and let Rob take Phillip out of his car seat and back into the house.

Little did I know, as Mom told me later, seeing as we had been unsuccessful in finding childcare, it had actually been Rob's suggestion, not Mom's, that they babysit Phillip for several hours every day while I worked. Those hours were going to turn into years of commitment, concern, and a love I didn't know Rob was even capable of displaying—or feeling.

Before Phillip started public school, the occupational, physical, and speech therapists made their weekly visits to my mom's house, given that Phillip spent most of his time with Mom and Rob while

Walter and I were at work. Rob not only made certain to be at home and present for all therapy consultations, but he took notes, asked questions, tested out exercises, and made suggestions to the therapists for improving methods. Rob would then schedule daily exercise routines, which he would practice with Phillip unfailingly. In between exercise sessions, Rob would hold, entertain, rock, feed, and just plain cuddle Phillip. Whenever I came to pick up my baby, Rob would relate details of Phillip's therapeutic progress, complete with meticulous demonstrations, and present me with diagrammed notes explaining exercises I needed to continue with Phillip at home.

As Phillip began to grow and develop, make eye contact, babble, and smile, I saw a continued change in, not only my baby, but my stepfather. Rob, stoic and humorless, became Papa, grinning and playful. Previously always on the recliner reading nature magazines and watching PBS, he de-evolved, crawling on the floor like a youngster himself, rolling a ball, or playing cars. And he started laughing. Smiling and laughing.

What is it about Phillip that Papa loves, feels attracted to, wants to be near? My mom wondered if Rob felt bad that Phillip might have been unwanted. Perhaps Rob has a natural attraction to adopted children since his own daughter was adopted by him. The reasons for the bond, however, are unimportant. The two have become best buddies. When they're apart for the weekend, Mom tells me that Rob will often muse, "I wonder what Phillip is doing right now." Now that Phillip is older and ambulatory, when the two of them meet up on a Monday after being separated all weekend, Phillip will run across the front yard yelling, "Papa!" Rob steps onto the front porch and they'll race toward each other, hug, and start playing. Their grandfather-grandson bond warms my heart.

Papa is in his 80s now. After years of paragliding and repelling, he has finally started showing the first signs of slowing down. Mom told me once while we were sitting across from each other in a booth at a Robinson Hills restaurant that Rob was having some medical problems and she was beginning to get worried. I thought, for the first time, about Rob's mortality, and I felt myself begin to cry. I imagined someday having to explain to Phillip that the most beloved person in his life, second only to Daddy, isn't here anymore. Phillip brought out the best in Papa, and softened my heart toward Rob. And Rob is my son's best friend. If my wish comes true, Rob will be here when he's 94 to see his best buddy graduate from high school.

Chapter 20:

Work

The family was busily falling in love with Phillip, but he still was not an official Cavilry. We had much to do before that could happen. The relief I felt after the 30-day period was great, but sadly that relief was not long lived. Shortly after the post-30-days celebratory shower, we were contacted by a social worker in Whittier and asked to make an appointment for her to come to our home, meet Phillip, and inspect our house. She also mailed a very long and very familiar list of documents we needed to collect. Over the next several months, we were required to have numerous interviews with this state-appointed social worker, often at our home, sometimes in her office an hour and a half away, always with Phillip present. The social worker also conducted interviews with other family members and a personal reference, and collected letters from several other personal references as well. Between appointments, the social worker was often busy with other adoption cases or waiting for our paperwork to be processed with the state. Weeks and sometimes months would go by between each stage of interviews, and every time three months passed, we would have to meet with her again in order for her to make certain that Phillip was still healthy and happy in his not-yet-approved new home. The process was long and tedious, resulting in a lot of vacation days from work.

Someday, if the arduous adoption process ever reached a conclusion, the birth certificate of Caden Michael Greene, parents Loretta and Timothy Greene, would be destroyed. A new birth certificate would be generated for Jonathon Phillip Cavilry, parents Rufina Sarah-Jane and Walter Scott Cavilry. I had a twinge of desire to acquire a copy of the first certificate—we were not permitted a copy—for Phillip's own personal interest and history, but I also longed for the end of the lengthy adoption process, the new birth certificate, and the assurance that Phillip had become, officially and forever, "ours".

As far as this new round of paperwork was concerned, I felt like we had already been through the same process 100 times, and Walter mentioned this, in passing, during one of our many interviews with the state social worker. She was surprised to find out that we had a completed home study. As a result, she asked for a copy of the study rather than gathering information a second time. I was frustrated by the lack of communication—once again. But finally, after a year and a half, the social worker recommended us for adoption and sent our paperwork to Sacramento for approval and finalization.

In the meantime, Betsy told me during one of our phone conversations that she had opened a bedroom door in Loretta's house. The door was always kept closed, and Betsy was curious to see what was in there. She found clothes, a bed, furniture, and decorations for a boy—but this was not Freddie's room. Loretta had kept a bedroom full of belongings for Freddie's baby brother, Caden, our Phillip.

When Betsy confronted Loretta about the sequestered items, scolding, "Phillip could have used all these things," Loretta sighed and admitted, "I just didn't know what to do."

A shiver went down my spine at the surreal feeling of my son's spirit residing across the state. Phillip is still in his birth mother's heart—I already knew that—but I didn't know that a ghost of his past self had retained residence in Loretta's house. Their connection was closer than I had known.

Chapter 21:

Heart

From the first day I learned of his existence, I knew of Phillip's heart defect and the fact that he would need surgery. This prior knowledge allowed our family the time to emotionally prepare and to find the best heart doctors available to treat him. We were referred to a more-than-qualified pediatric cardiologist, Dr. Leonard Singh in Ten Acres, very close to our home.

I don't think we could have traveled the country and found a doctor who was more qualified. Dr. Singh was able to explain Phillip's specific heart condition—tetralogy of Fallot—in simple enough terms that Walter and I could define the disease clearly for curious and concerned family members. And Dr. Singh had experience treating numerous patients with Down syndrome who had the same or similar heart condition as Phillip.

The defects present in tetralogy of Fallot caused blood to enter Phillip's heart but return to the system without being nourished with oxygen by the pulmonary artery. The resulting deprivation of oxygen to the brain caused Phillip to be listless, easily tired, and sometimes to have a mottled appearance to his skin. When all factors are healthy, a person's blood oxygen level should be close to 100%. Phillip's was usually around 78%—not ideal, but not horrible. So, Dr. Singh hoped that we could wait and plan the surgery for when Phillip was bigger and stronger, around 6 months old.

Often, my community interpreting assignments would require that I drive an hour or longer to unfamiliar cities. With finances pulled thin, I went willingly to where the money was. I don't much enjoy having to travel more than a few miles from home, but since I was available all day and the kids were with my mom, I went on an eight-hour interpreting assignment in Northland. The drive was over an hour and a half each way, but the length of the full-day interpreting task made the travel worthwhile.

For any interpreting assignment over two hours in length, two interpreters are scheduled to work together, relieving each other at fixed intervals of about 20 minutes to avoid fatigue or repetitive-motion injury. Being in an area of southern California I'd never seen before, and since I am, as previously detailed, directionally challenged, I quickly became lost. In Northland but unable to find the assignment, I pulled over and sent a text to my team interpreter.

"I'm lost, but hope to be there soon."

My team immediately texted back, "I'm already here with a team! Were you told to come here today?"

After some detective work with the two interpreters and our supervisor, we discovered that the interpreting agency had hired one too many interpreters for the assignment. My supervisors were the ones in error, and because I couldn't be expected to find another job for the day with such a late plan change, I would still be paid for the entire day. But since my presence was unnecessary, the interpreters and the agency decided I should be the one sent back home because I had the farthest drive. So, immediately after my arrival, without even exiting my car, I turned around and headed right back toward home.

Shortly merging back onto the freeway, I got a call. I answered the phone via GPS. A very businesslike voice began, "Hello Ms. Cavilry, this is the receptionist from Dr. Singh's office. Your mother and the doctor are walking Jonathon over to the hospital right now."

I felt the blood plummet from my face like a boulder off a cliff.

Panicking, I loudly blurted, "What's wrong?"

The receptionist's reply was, "*I* don't know what's *wrong*." I think—I hope—she quickly caught the lack of bedside manner in her response, because she immediately went on, "Jonathon's oxygen levels were much lower than usual, so the doctor decided he needs to be checked into the hospital for surgery right away." Dr. Singh was great, but I never did like that receptionist. However the present moment wasn't the time to brood on her lack of professionalism (and her insistence on *not* calling him Phillip). I let my foot rest more heavily on the gas pedal.

As I drove a little faster, I called Walter to let him know that he would need to leave work pretty soon. He called Grandpa and

GrandMinnie to let them know what was happening, and I called Mom to say I was on the way. Familial duties completed, I settled into the one-and-a-half hour journey as quickly and safely as possible to our neighborhood hospital.

I had always known the day of his surgery would come, but I thought it was going to be when he was six months old, not three. I was terrified. Instead of bringing Phillip to the hospital at a pre-arranged appointment time, he was being rushed in on an emergency basis. And so small. I was imagining his tiny body being moved to rooms and places he wasn't familiar with and didn't understand, lying on a stretcher rather than on a mommy or grandmommy's lap. I drove a little faster.

Pulling into the hospital parking structure and depositing my car into the first empty spot I found, I walked briskly through the lot, into the building, to the front desk and told the volunteer that I was there for my infant son. The receptionist picked up the phone and announced, "The mother is here." I was expected.

The volunteer directed me to the doorway of a room which was whirling with of a swarm of doctors and nurses buzzing around a full-size adult's hospital bed, and my tiny baby being held down in the middle of the mattress having an IV inserted into his scalp.

Mom met me at the doorway and gave me a much-needed and long hug. I was glad to have my mommy with me at that moment, and I briefly reverted to childhood, letting her pat me on the back with maternal comfort. I'm sure Phillip could have used a hug from his mommy as well.

When Mom released herself from my embrace, she explained what had happened to bring Phillip so quickly and unexpectedly to his present situation.

Shortly after I dropped the kids off at my mom's house that morning, she noted that Phillip's skin was looking a little more mottled and blue than usual. Soon, he started to show some difficulty breathing, until he actually started to pant, noticeably unable to catch his breath. Mom called Dr. Singh's office, described the symptoms, and was instructed to bring Phillip in immediately for a check-up. Grandmother and baby, Heidi in tow, were in the doctor's waiting room within half an hour.

In Dr. Singh's examination room, the nurse performed a standard check of Phillip's blood oxygen level. It was down into the 60s. Immediately, Dr. Singh retrieved an oxygen tank and placed a little child-sized nasal cannula under Phillip's nose, allowing him to receive as much direct, pure oxygen as possible. Moving quickly, Dr. Singh, wheeling the oxygen tank behind him, raced out of his office building, through the parking lot, to Pine Valley Hospital, Mom trotting behind holding Phillip, Heidi clinging to her arm repeating, "I'm hungry. Grammy, I'm hungry." When they got to the hospital, a nurse took Heidi into a waiting room and fed her a cafeteria meal while Mom stayed with Phillip.

Phillip needed to get care as soon as possible, so the plan was to transport Phillip from Pine Valley to Beverly Hills Children's Hospital via helicopter. The traffic was too heavy to risk the extra time spent in an ambulance on an LA rush-hour freeway.

When his scalp IV was in place, the doctors and nurses left the room, allowing me to rush to Phillip's side. I slipped my arm under his neck and leaned over the bed to give him as many hugs and kisses as possible, talking and cooing with him, nose to nose, only looking away from his gaze if a monitor alarm sounded, indicating that his blood oxygen level had taken a nosedive. I gave my son as much attention as possible, but was very much aware of the alarm, which rang every minute or less. I would be hearing that alarm with attentive, silent panic, my chest tightening with each sound, almost every minute for the next ten days.

Far too soon, I heard a distant chopping noise; a nurse came into the room to announce, "There's the helicopter."

My heart jumped in my chest. Several attendants were required to accompany Phillip on the already-tight quarters of the aircraft; there was no room for me to escort my son on his flight. Hearing the approaching rotor blades slicing the air in rapid, repeating, surprisingly loud chops, I envisioned my tiny, innocent three-month-old baby boy, eyes wide with confusion, body a twisting highway of tubes and needles, surrounded by paramedics, high above the ground, with no concept of what was happening to him. I tightened my arm around his shoulders, leaned across his body, and pressed my cheek against his.

In an instant, the room was filled with paramedics maneuvering a large stretcher. One attendant who, I'm certain, could see the wide-eyed dread on my contorted face told me, "You can walk with us until we're about to go up to the landing pad. Then you can say goodbye from there."

I was grateful. While the emergency crew adjusted, moved, plugged and unplugged, I was allowed to remain by Phillip's side, holding his hand and talking to him.

With my infant boy on the man-sized stretcher, the paramedics and I walked out of the room, past the nurse's station, through the automatic double door, and into the parking garage. We went down a short walkway and around the corner when, far too soon, one of the paramedics regretfully informed me, "Now we'll take your son up in the elevator to the landing pad. You can give him a kiss good-bye here."

I looked down at my baby boy, who suddenly looked even tinier on that enormous stretcher. I leaned over and kissed him on both cheeks, looked into this eyes and bubbled, "You're going on a helicopter ride! It's going to be so fun! I'll meet you when you're done. Okay? I love you, baby. I love you."

He looked up at me, his eyes wide, his mouth set. Motionless, arms at his sides, unblinking, his gaze never left my face. As the paramedics began moving into the elevator, the foot of the stretcher going through the doors first, Phillip slowly tilted his chin upward, enabling him to look up over his shoulder, keeping his eyes fixed on mine as the physical distance between us grew.

"Bye, baby! Have fun! Bye!" I called and waved, but he merely watched, craning his neck and maintaining his stare, until he, bright-red hair last, disappeared into the elevator.

The doors glided shut and I burst into tears. Shoulders hunched over and shuddering, I walked to my car.

As soon as I steered my Corolla out of the parking structure, I called Walter and told him to leave work and head to Beverly Hills. Since he works in Mar Vista, he would, most likely, get to the hospital before me to join Phillip in the NICU. I was glad that a family member would be there to greet Phillip shortly after the helicopter's arrival.

I breathed deeply and settled into highway-101 traffic. While I drove, I thought of my son, high above me, and I wished for a flying DeLorean to take me to Beverly Hills before him. How confused he must have been in the air with strangers on such a loud, close aircraft—and how scared.

After about 20 minutes, one of the helicopter paramedics called to let me know that they had arrived safely at Beverly Hills Children's Hospital and Phillip was being admitted. I was grateful to know that his tiny body was done soaring above the skies, but I envisioned him now being bustled about, hooked up, poked at, with no familiar faces anywhere. Before I could worry too long, Walter called to say he had arrived at BHCH and was with Phillip in the NICU. I exhaled—but didn't relax completely. Phillip was now with Daddy, a familiar, loving face, but he wasn't with me. I had an indescribable need, an involuntary tugging in my chest, pulling me toward him. Freeway rush-hour traffic forced me into an involuntary game of tug o' war with my son. Motherly instinct was turned up several extra notches.

When I finally got to BHCH, parked my car and located the NICU, I found my son, once again, lying on a large hospital bed, beeping monitors surrounding him. An IV was already in Phillip's little arm, which was splinted straight to prevent him from bending at the elbow and disturbing the inserted tubing. A pulse oximeter was taped to his big toe to monitor his heartbeat as well as blood oxygen saturation, which continued to take regular dips below safe numbers. Each time the oxygen levels plummeted, nurses would saunter up as calmly as possible and hold a large plastic tube in front of Phillip's mouth and nose, providing him with even more oxygen, in addition to the constant release of oxygen from the cannula taped above his upper lip. But it wasn't long before the medical staff realized that a huge concentration of oxygen really didn't matter—Phillip's heart was not circulating oxygen-rich blood properly; he would remain oxygen-deprived, no matter how much air the nurses blew directly into his face. The oxygen was just not reaching his brain. He needed his heart operation.

My baby looked so uncomfortable, wrapped in twists of plastic, metal, and tape, like a dolphin stuck in a tuna net. I wanted to get him out of the hospital and into his home as soon as I could. But shortly, I found out that, due to a little stuffiness, the surgeons had decided to postpone Phillip's operation until his sinuses were a little clearer. So Phillip would have to remain in the hospital, perpetually oxygen deprived, for several days before he could have the operation that would save his life. As much as we could, we made ourselves comfortable and settled in to wait.

Mom wanted to brighten up Phillip's white, joyless hospital crib a little bit, so she brought in a mobile her friend, Edith, had made. Edith was a woman in her 80s who danced with my mom and me in some local folk-dancing groups. The tradition was that, whenever a grandchild was born to one of the fellow folk dancers, Edith would crochet and gift one of these mobiles. The mobile consisted of about 10 yarn balls, each one of a different solid color, a long crocheted chain stretching from each bright orb, all gathered up and tied together at the end in a knot. A simple toy, but very attractive to the kiddies. When Heidi was born, we received a mobile for her, and when Phillip joined the Cavilrys, he got a brand-new mobile of his own. So, when Mom wanted to decorate the hospital crib, she thought the Edith-Mobile a perfect, colorful decorative element.

When Phillip had a back-facing car seat, before he was even able to move his arms, he used to giggle while we drove. At a couple of months old, he discovered arm movement. He used to straighten one elbow, raise his fist above his head, and babble at his clenched fingers. He never took to a pacifier or sucked his thumb, but when he was tired or relaxed, he would suck the side of his hand at the pudgy bulge below the base of his thumb. But with Phillip's favorite waving-fist splinted and his thumb pudge unable to be sucked, he was in need of some self-comfort while in the NICU. The moment my mom hung up the mobile on the light above the crib, Phillip's eyes widened, his pupils focused on the colorful orbs dangling above him, his mouth grew into a big grin, and he began babbling and babbling as if talking to an old, beloved friend. His joy with the rainbow spheres was so great and his smiling and talking so profound, we couldn't help but laugh and exclaim to each other, "We have to tell Edith!" We took pictures of Phillip smiling at the mobile, and Mom made a phone call to let the maker know her toy was being put to good use. Edith was very pleased.

Even replete with blue skin, Phillip stole the show at the NICU. There were at least 10 nurses who became acquainted with him, and each one loved our little boy. I heard, more than once, "When I saw that I was assigned to work with Phillip this shift, I was so happy! I'm going to hold him all night."

At the time, BHCH was waiting to be moved to a new location, and the current quarters were wanting in many aspects of comfort and décor. We were told repeatedly that the new NICU would be gorgeous. That didn't make us feel too much better. The NICU we were dealing with in the present was packed almost bed to bed with monitors and mechanisms all around, leaving barely enough room for one small crib-side chair. As a result, there was no space. Parents were not allowed to spend the night at the bedside of their ailing babies. Removing myself from Phillip's side every evening was like removing my heart from my chest. At least I felt safe leaving him in the care of the BHCH nurses. Not only did they do a great job of giving care, they also really seemed to enjoy my son's presence.

I spent as much time as I could at BHCH. Whenever possible, I would arrive at 6:00 or 7:00 AM, stay until midnight, spend the night on the couch of nearby friends Atusa and Sam, and then wake up early to go back again to the NICU.

We were in grave need of the money, so I occasionally tried to go to work. On those days, Mom, Rob, or Walter would be assigned vigil at Phillip's bedside. We made certain that Phillip always had a familiar face to give him comfort in this strange, inexplicable situation.

With Phillip in the hospital and our minds constantly occupied with scheduling, planning, and worrying, our attention to Heidi was severely inadequate. Even worse, very shortly after Phillip was admitted to the hospital, Heidi's first day of kindergarten arrived. Walter, my mom, and I actively put Phillip's situation out of our minds for a few moments to dress up our girl, take pictures, and wave Heidi off for her big day. We were all torn and distracted, but did our best to, over the next several days, create pockets of availability to have special alone-time with Heidi, alternating turns being Phillip's familiar face for the evening. Although we tried, our parenting of Heidi was most certainly insufficient while Phillip remained hospitalized.

By the time four or five days of Phillip-watch had passed, we all became much more accustomed to the sound of monitor alarms.

Although we would look with attention at the numbers on the display each time beeping commenced, our looks were much less panicked and much more habitual. When Phillip's oxygen saturation took a severe nosedive, a British nurse with a smooth English accent liltingly sang "Everything's okay...except...for your sats...of 12." Her voice was soothing, and she spoke like she was narrating the sweet words of a children's books. It didn't matter that Phillip was being told, in reality, "Your situation is actually pretty dire." He just liked the sing-songy voice and the nice lady accompanying it. Phillip responded with a pleasant smile and a weakening coo, eyes becoming more and more cartoonishly crossed, and although my son was nearly passing out, I couldn't help but giggle. As the moments of concerning oxygen levels were so constant, his situation was difficult to watch. But he was in one of the best hospitals in the world, under constant observation by experts in the field of pediatric medicine. I was learning to become, although concerned, relaxed.

At times, his blood oxygen saturation would become so low, the monitor would not read a numerical percentage, but merely an "XX". I would inwardly panic as nurses would rush to the bedside and Phillip would begin to feebly babble, his eyes unfocused, smiling in an oxygen-deprivation-induced high. I stepped back and trusted the nurses.

The weekend came, and although Phillip's sinuses were clearer, the surgeon had the weekend off, continuing the family's bedside vigil an additional two days. On Sunday, Walter and I took time to walk around Los Angeles with Heidi and our friend, my comforting and tiny coworker Anna, shop for something frivolous at a toy store, and go to a movie. Heidi enjoyed the uninterrupted attention of her parents and friend, and we were momentarily relieved of the accrued guilt from having neglected our daughter for the past several days.

Relaxed, recharged, and prepared, we were ready for Monday— operation day. Before surgery, Phillip needed to have a new IV placed in his arm. His small veins, nervously retreating from view, were impossible to find. But they needed to come out of hiding, voluntarily or not. Thus began the agonizing search for a willing vein. The nurses suggested that relatives not comfort him during the procedure to avoid associating family members with any painful medical processes, rather saving that relationship for comforting moments afterward.

My mother and I sat to the side while my baby was surrounded by a roomful of medical professionals, all bracing, groping, and poking my child. The first stick of the needle brought Phillip's screams, and his verbal demonstration of pain didn't stop for the full 20 minutes we sat in the chairs next to his bed. I put my head on my mother's shoulder and wished for a vein to voluntarily step forward.

Eventually, a nurse suggested that Mom and I leave and wait in a small room off the hallway, as listening to my son's screams was surely heart wrenching for us, and our physical presence was of no use. I concurred and we left the NICU, went down the hall, and found the tiny four-seat waiting room. We sat and waited, trying to chat but finding conversation difficult to come by since we could still hear Phillip's mournful howls every time the NICU doors swung open. The nurse came to retrieve us as soon as a vein was found and an IV put in place, two hours after they had first started searching and jabbing. Getting the green light to return, I immediately ran and replanted myself at Phillip's bedside to hold his hand while he, exhausted, slept.

The next morning arrived, and I had extremely mixed emotions. Phillip would finally undergo the procedure to save him from constant oxygen deprivation, but he would also be having major, life-threatening surgery. My emotional stress was great, thinking of Phillip's pristine, smooth, soft, untouched chest being cut and pried open, permanently and radically scarred. His childish perfection would be irrevocably compromised. And, of course, there would be risks. I tried hard not to think about the possibility of death, concentrating only on the healing oxygen that my boy's brain would finally benefit from.

There were several structures in Phillip's heart that needed mending, but the most vital was the repairing of the pulmonary artery to increase flow of oxygenated blood to the body. As he had been through so much physical trauma during the last week—severely and repeatedly oxygen deprived, day and night, for several days—the heart surgeon wasn't sure whether or not he would be able to complete the entire four-part repair of the tetralogy of Fallot in one operation. To summarize, this upcoming heart surgery might not be Phillip's last. I kept my fingers crossed and hoped that all the repairs could be completed in one operation—I dreaded the thought of my son's chest being opened twice.

My mom stayed at home, the plan being that she would spend the day with Heidi, taking her to school, picking her up, and having special grandmother-granddaughter time in the evening. In the meantime, Walter and I woke up early and made our way to Beverly Hills before 6:00 AM to spend some time with Phillip before his big moment. We held him, kissed him, and loved him when, all too soon, the doctors came to take our baby into surgery. We both kissed him one more time; he watched us with the same curious eyes as he had before the helicopter ride. Lying on his back while his bed was wheeled away, through double doors and down a bright white hallway, he craned his neck and tilted his head to stare into my eyes as long as physics would allow, silently asking me where he was going. When the gurney and my boy disappeared from sight, I turned to Walter and cried, my head on his shoulder, in anticipation of a very long day.

My father and stepmother came to the hospital to emotionally support us while we waited. We all sat together in the large, unentertaining waiting room. The space held five or six low, rectangular coffee tables, each one surrounded on three sides by 12 identical, square, unergonomic brown chairs. The fourth side of each table faced the room's center walkway, which ran the length of the room from entrance to exit. An uninteresting wooden front desk was to the side of the doubled-doored egress. There was no television or any pictures on the walls. And everything was brown. Brown carpet, brown chairs, and brown coffee tables. Memory tells me that the walls and ceiling were also brown, but that memory might be due to my feelings of the day—pretty colorless. I had several light books with me as well as some crocheting supplies, but I was unable to concentrate on anything but the seemingly-brown wall across from me and my blue baby so far away.

After more than an hour of silent, inactive sitting, lifting not so much as a scrap of yarn or reading a single paragraph, I received a call on the phone at the waiting-room front desk. When I heard the receptionist call my name, I ran to answer the phone, feeling a twinge of panic—why was I being summoned?

"Hello?" I answered, a little out of breath, heart just short of pounding.

"Hi, Mrs. Cavilry. This is the operation room nurse. Doctor McMann wanted to let you know that the first incision has been made."

My head swam. I envisioned my son lying on the operating table, cut open, bleeding, chest gaping, organs exposed.

"Oh, okay," I muttered. I didn't know what else to say. I thanked her for the information, hung up, and went back to sit by my family.

"They just wanted to let us know that they've made the first incision."

Seeing my pallid visage, my stepmother offered, "I guess they just want you to know that everything is going as planned."

"I suppose," I responded, trying to be understanding. My cheeks must not have regained any color, because soon my stepmother added,

"Why don't you and Walter go for a walk? We have at least four or five hours. The two of you can go get breakfast."

I didn't want to leave the room, preferring to simply sit and obsess about my son's current predicament. But rather than watch his wife go slowly insane with anxiety, Walter took my arm and guided me outside.

Walter and I spent the next several hours with Dad and Bea taking turns getting coffee, looking in the gift shop, sitting in the lobby, and getting more coffee. I was thankful to my dad for staying such a long time—over six hours—to emotionally support his daughter and his namesake.

None too soon, when we had all reconvened in the lobby, we were called once again by the operating-room nurse, this time to let us know that Phillip's chest was closed and he was in recovery. We were asked to go to the small waiting room on the sixth floor in preparation for the doctor to come talk to us. We rapidly and obediently did as we were told.

After we got off the elevator, we sat in a small room with no windows, another waiting family, and a television that was playing who-knows-what—something in Spanish. The wait was probably quite brief, but it felt very drawn out—I was anticipating information of how the operation had gone and, even though certainly nothing had gone wrong, I expected bad news. The possibility of being told that the operation had ended in a last-minute tragedy was nil at this point, but the long day and the stress of knowing what my son was going through had weakened my sensibilities to some extent—I worried that my child had surprisingly died on the operating table and I was waiting, while listening to a Mexican soap opera, to be informed of this fact.

However, after about 20 minutes of anticipation, the heart surgeon came into the gloomy space to shine some light on the situation and on my darkened outlook. His dignified European face appearing drawn and tired under his 5:00 shadow, he shook our hands before quietly leading us through a short recap of the day's procedure.

He concluded with the most important phrase, "The operation was very successful."

Phillip was stable and doing well in the recovery room. I hoped that meant he wouldn't need to come back for another operation. But Dr. McMann went on, "Due to the stress that your son's heart has gone through in the past few days, I decided it would be better to only repair the pulmonary artery now, let him rest and grow stronger, and then fix the rest of the heart defects in about six months."

My heart sank. The relief I was feeling went away with the knowledge that this was all going to have to happen again. I was dejected, but took the news with as much bravery as I could muster. The past week had been so difficult for our three-month-old boy, so the doctor wanted to put as little strain on Phillip's tiny body as possible. As a result, the rerouting of the pulmonary artery was done without stopping the heart—with skillful, steady hands, the doctor had repaired the defect while Phillip's heart continued to beat in his chest. We were very impressed, very grateful, and, although disappointed, very optimistic. Phillip did it once; we could help him do it again. And I thought of Loretta briefly when I said to myself, *I need to prove that I* can *handle Phillip's heart surgery, even if I have to handle it twice.*

After several more minutes, a nurse called to report that they had finished with their post-operative procedures and we could visit Phillip. Walter and I were led to our boy's bedside to see him sleeping, intubated and bandaged. I longed to hold him, but was unable to so soon after surgery. Phillip was heavily medicated, forcing him to rest and recover. The nurse thus suggested that Walter and I go home for a solid night's sleep, as the upcoming days might be a little rough. I hated to leave my baby's side, but I knew my presence would do him no good; my closeness would be much more appreciated by Heidi. I opted to leave my love and thoughts with Phillip and go cuddle up with my daughter and husband instead. We went home.

That evening, Walter and I gave Heidi some extra love and attention. She'd been a trooper during the past week's neglect, and she would have more abandonment in the remaining days of Phillip's hospitalization. We let her know what was going on, what her brother was going through, and that we appreciated her so much for her strength and understanding. At bedtime, we all slept together in Mommy and Daddy's bed, giving Heidi the additional parental proximity and comfort that she surely needed.

Phillip's recovery was, understandably, very painful. After a full night of rest, I returned to his morning bedside to see him swollen, intubated, full of drainage tubes, and uncomfortable. To prevent Phillip tugging on any tubes or wires, his hands were both strapped down to the bed with a soft white cloth. His breathing tube prevented him from vocalizing, but his expression told me that, if he could, he would be crying. All I wanted to do was hold and comfort him, and I'm sure all he wanted was some comfortable holding, but he couldn't be moved while the breathing tube was in place. I leaned over him, avoided sensitive equipment and painful body parts, and stroked his hair, helpless to give him any additional form of consolation. He looked at my eyes and silently wept.

I remember helplessly watching him suffer through a case of painful hiccups. With each mocking spasm of his diaphragm, he would contort his body and face in a visible display of agony. I willed the clock to speed through his period of recovery.

Doctors were constantly coming to check on various aspects of Phillip's condition, and to inquire if I had any questions. Each time they came into Phillip's room, the BHCH doctors and nurses were wonderful about asking if we had any questions. I rarely had anything to ask, but I was always grateful for that considerate aspect of the their bedside manners. However, whenever Walter was present for a doctor's visit, he would shower the physician with questions about the technical details of Phillip's surgery. As a result, Walter knows all about exactly what was done to our son's circulatory system, and he can recite all the ins and outs, twists and turns, and ups and downs of tetralogy of Fallot. I know that the syndrome, which has four defects in conjunction, was discovered by a Dr. Fallot, and I can spell the condition properly. But someday, when Phillip wants to know precisely why he has a scar on his chest, I'll have to respond, "Ask Daddy."

No longer in the NICU, one parent was permitted to spend the night at Phillip's bedside, reclining in a large leather-ish easy chair. I went to work when community interpreting assignments came up, and Walter worked every evening, so we created a schedule of availability with Mom, one or two of us at BHCH every day, and either Walter or I spending every night.

The nights when I was scheduled to go home were the most difficult. Bedtime, for me, has always been the time when my motherly instincts kick into high gear, singing to, holding, and protecting my babies in the dark of night. Knowing that Heidi was safe in our familiar and comfortable house, I wanted desperately to stay in the hospital every evening with Phillip. However, my husband also had the same desire to stay with his son. On those evenings when I left Phillip in Walter's care, I would go home to spend some time with Heidi, bear a sleepless night, take Heidi to school the next morning, and speed back to Beverly Hills at the first moment's availability. I was trying to be a good mom to both of my kids, but my heart was drawn to the one with the sutured chest. I kept communication open with my daughter and tried to help her understand my plight. She was an absolute gem and gave me all the understanding that her five-year-old mentality could muster. I was very proud of her.

After a few days, the doctors decided it was safe to remove Phillip's breathing tube. The removal process was brief but uncomfortable—when the doctor pulled the tube out of Phillip's esophagus, my baby opened his mouth, thrust out his tongue, furrowed his brow with enough horizontal wrinkles to put a 100-year-old man to shame, and coughed in a display of ultimate discomfort. However, as soon as the doctor was certain that Phillip was breathing well on his own, I was finally able to hold my son. The nurse brought a rocking chair into the room—I sat down, a pillow under my arm, and was handed my beautiful baby. He still had a drainage tube in his abdomen, an oxygen supply at his nose, and a pulse oximeter on his toe, but I let the nurses organize the pathways of cords and lines while I concentrated on cradling my baby's head in the crook of my elbow and looking right into his big blue eyes, kissing his tiny nose repeatedly. Comforted in my arms, he soon fell asleep. I continued holding his sleeping, warm body, making up for lost time.

While my mom and I sat next to Phillip's crib one afternoon, a young woman in a hospital uniform came into our room and asked, "Do you need any toys or books?"

I wasn't exactly sure what she meant. Did she want us to buy them? Phillip hadn't yet developed the ability to request specific toys and he couldn't read, so I merely stammered, "Um…I don't know!" We all laughed.

She glanced over at Phillip and, viewing his age and condition, offered, "Does he like music or stuffed animals? Or maybe picture books?" She probably saw Mom and I look questioningly at each other, because she added, "They're a donation—he can take them home."

This freed my mind to think a bit more creatively and gratefully. "Well, he likes lights and music. He doesn't really seem to care about stuffed animals or books."

"Maybe a mobile?" Remembering Phillip's infatuation with the Edith-Mobile, we liked this offer. The volunteer left and came back with an armful of toys. First was a musical mobile with three fat, colorful fish that dangled down from the domed music box at the center, and star-shaped openings covering the top that, when the light was switched on, would shine a rotating galaxy on the ceiling. She also gave us a music box that attached to the side of the crib and displayed gentle, flashing lights. Lastly, she gave Phillip a mirror with a magnetic plastic mouse that ran in circles on the shiny, reflective surface. The volunteer stayed and helped us install all of the new treasures on the metal bars of Phillip's hospital crib. Along with Edith's crocheted creation, Phillip's crib was quite festive. I was very touched by this donation program at BHCH, and I wondered if the toys and books helped the other child patients feel a little happiness during their stays in this hospital as well.

The living conditions for nighttime sleepovers in the hospital were pretty uncomfortable—the only restroom was a single-stalled unit down the hall that was shared by all parents and visitors. The vinyl-covered recliners that we slept on didn't exactly allow the skin to breathe. In fact, they were veritable sweat factories. I made the situation worse by being emotionally unable to leave my boy in the crib at night, opting instead to hold his hot body in my arms all night long. The combination of Phillip's added body heat and the rubbery recliner on my butt throughout the night, and the lack of bathing facilities resulted in a wicked case of heat rash on the backs of my legs. But I just couldn't put my baby in his bed; I held on to Phillip all night, and ignored my current medical situation. I proved myself a very devoted mom.

Phillip shared his hospital room with a six-year-old boy who had just gone through a kidney transplant. The unfortunate child was miserable—in pain, confined, and probably confused. He was heavily medicated, but during the times that I visited with Phillip, I don't remember that poor boy sleeping much at all. He wanted to sit in his mother's lap, but he couldn't get comfortable. He wanted to eat, but he felt dreadful. He wanted to watch a movie, but he couldn't concentrate through the discomfort. He wanted to play, but his own drainage tube got in the way. He was once given permission to go with his mother to the floor's playroom for young patients. When asked if he wanted to go, through his moans and whines, the boy uttered that he did indeed want to go play. While his mother and the nurse moved and adjusted the child's IV, the poor little boy, trying to be a helpful little trooper, tearfully asked, "I should carry this?" as he gently picked up the baby-bottle-sized container which caught the fluid draining through the tube trailing from a hole in his abdomen. He was miserable, and the drainage tube probably made him very uncomfortable, but he wanted so much to be a happy kid enjoying toys in a playroom. I also remember when he fell asleep on his mother's lap and suddenly jumped up, dreaming, yet screaming and biting, in a medication-induced aggressive attack. He immediately fell back to sleep and surely didn't remember the incident (I did pity the mother and the bite marks on her arm.) Although that moment was visually and audibly much more striking, much worse and more permanently etched in my memory is the sound of that poor little boy's voice when he held the drainage bottle and wept, "I should carry this?" trying to be helpful through his tears so that he could go play. At the time and to this day, I wish him speedy healing and a comfortable, healthy, long life…with lots of playing.

Phillip was recovering well, but had additional difficult moments ahead of him. There was wound cleaning and physical therapy, but worst of all was the removal of the drainage tube in his abdomen. The thick, clear plastic tube went directly from a hole in his belly, over the side of the crib, and into a large plastic container about the size of a cereal box, catching all of the fluid that drained out of him after the operation. I tried never to look at the entrance site on his tummy—it gave me the willies. I hated having to pick Phillip up and move him around with that long tube wiggling around, as it surely must have been uncomfortable.

For Phillip's tube to be removed, it had to be slowly and carefully pulled out by a doctor, and then the resulting hole in his skin stitched closed. The procedure sounded pretty uncomfortable to me, but I was eager for it to be done, as its removal was certain to give him more comfort and freedom. So, I remained in the room for the removal process that was, thankfully, brief, with very little crying involved (his or mine). As soon as I was given the okay, I rushed to the crib and scooped up my baby, the remaining tubes and cords merely for monitoring his vital signs—superficially attached, non-invasive. Still taking care to avoid the center of his chest, I was much more at ease to cuddle my little Phillip, put him down, and pass him around during daily visits from Daddy, Grammy and Papa, Grandma and Grandpa, and GrandMinnie. We were all able to enjoy him a bit more.

One morning when I was holding Phillip in my lap, a doctor came into Phillip's room. After traditional perfunctory greetings, he asked, "How would you like to take Phillip home today?"

All of the doctors and nurses had been loving and wonderful with my precious son, and so amazingly attentive to our every need, whether or not our requests for assistance were actually voiced. I was extremely grateful to all of them for treating my son with such care, dedication, and true concern. However, I couldn't wait to get out of there and take my baby home.

Walter sped away from work and brought Phillip's car seat in from the Camry. While Mom and I gathered up Phillip's belongings—hospital donations of new toys, books, games, and even the fishy mobile for his crib, as well as containers of formula, bottles and nipples, bandages and cleansing ointment—the attending nurse took a final reading of pulse, respiration, and blood pressure. Finally, we gently placed Phillip in the car seat and secured the straps, taking care to pad the chest clip with a blanket, cushioning the sensitive wound on his breastbone.

I felt a wave of excitement and relief as we carried Phillip to the front desk to say goodbye to the doctors and nurses we had met during our stay at BHCH. In the parking structure, after locking Phillip's car seat in place, we carefully drove out and began heading down the street, the hospital shrinking in the distance. It seemed like our little boy had been trapped in the hospital for weeks; in reality, it was only 10 days. Still, I was glad those 10 days were over.

As Walter turned the wheel, I quietly watched the 405 freeway approach. I was glad to be leaving Los Angeles, but my happiness was reserved. Phillip would take a few months to recover and heal, grow bigger and stronger, but I never forgot that he would have to return to BHCH once again for the completion of his heart repair. And the future surgery would be much more extensive. I certainly wasn't looking forward to it, for his sake or mine.

Chapter 22:

Improvement

It wasn't until we got home that I fully realized just how much a lack of oxygen had been affecting Phillip's behavior and development.

Phillip's eyes always had a sunken, dark appearance. Any time we had goal-setting meetings with his therapists, I always mentioned that I would like to find ways to help Phillip notice and react more to stimuli in his surroundings. He'd learned to look in our eyes and smile, but he'd still been fairly unresponsive to items such as toys and books.

After a good night's post-surgery sleep in our own home, I woke to find Daddy sitting on the bed with an open picture book, Melinda Long's *How I Became a Pirate*, slowly turning pages and talking about each drawing, while Phillip, lying on his back with his head turned toward the pages, smiled, vocalized, and giggled in response to each new image. He was smiling at and commenting on the pictures, reacting to each illustration, thoroughly enjoying the detailed expressions of the pirates. Seeing father and son interacting like this made me grateful for the time we had spent in the hospital. The operation brought about a brightness, an awareness to his face that had been previously absent. Phillip's forward developmental progression made me wonder if the second surgery was even necessary—but I left that to the experts to decide.

The additional oxygen to Phillip's body and brain didn't only bring about a leap in mental development but a physical one as well. It wasn't long before Phillip learned to hold and play with toys as well as to move about more freely. On October 4th while Papa was babysitting, he witnessed Phillip commemorate the anniversary of the launching of Sputnik by rolling over from front to back for the first time.

After six months of healing, growing, developing, and enriching our lives, it was time for Phillip to go back to BHCH for his second surgery. A hole had to be closed and a valve repaired (Phillip can ask Daddy for details later.) We had the benefit this time around of making an appointment for the procedure, which Phillip was polite enough to keep. We made plans with work and created schedules before going to the hospital, rather than panicked floundering.

This was also apparently the hospitalization of celebrity sightings. Walter and Heidi saw Dog the Bounty Hunter strut through the BHCH lobby, complete with black leather, chains, and sunglasses. Mom, Phillip and I shared a friendly, private elevator ride with a charming and personable Kelsey Grammar. (We won.)

Tensions were lighter, but still, when the day of the operation came, we arrived at the medical center burdened with an experienced awareness of what Phillip would be going through. And we knew beforehand that this operation would be more extensive and physically taxing. Phillip sat on the hospital gurney in the pre op area, laughing and playing between times of begging to be fed (he wasn't allowed food or drink before the surgery.) Phillip didn't want to leave my arms, but when the nurse offered a syringe of medicine, he was friendly enough with her to suck the blue liquid down like it was the tastiest breakfast he'd ever enjoyed—he immediately signed his demand for "more". When he wasn't allowed seconds, he tried to cry but soon didn't care—the medicine was something to relax and calm him before being taken to the operating room. He went googly-eyed and reached out to touch and explore the nurse's face. I handed Phillip over to the nurse's complete care, and my son didn't notice my absence as he was carried down the hallway and out of sight, me calling, "I love you, baby," as he rounded the corner and disappeared from sight.

Cue the crying mommy. I don't know that a mother can ever get used to sending her baby off to surgery.

Although we had supplied our daughter with books, toys, movies, and a laptop so that she could wait with us, when GrandMinnie made a surprise visit to the hospital waiting room to take Heidi out for the day, she happily dashed off with her grandmother for big-girl time—

manicures and shopping. Papa, Grammy, Walter and I settled ourselves in the lobby to watch Heidi's movies and begin the familiar wait.

I was aware, from experience, that we would be getting calls from the operating room to let us know of the steps being taken and the progress being made during the various surgical procedures. However, every time my name was called out to come to the phone at the front desk, I jumped up in panicked preparation for bad news. Running to the phone each time, my heart would race, and then hearing, "The first incision has been made," my head would swim with unsavory visions of the peeling and disemboweling of my son. I wished they wouldn't call us at all, letting us relax with the notion that everything was progressing as planned.

I especially didn't want to hear updates this time around since Phillip's heart had to be stopped and his blood circulated through his body via machine. My merciless brain created vivid images of Phillip spread-eagle on the operating table, heart in a metal pan at his side, his chest pinned open at four corners like something from *Hellraiser*. The thought of my baby's blood circulating mechanically reminded me of a bad dream I'd had years ago: All people, when they reached a certain age, were required to have their brains temporarily removed for the purpose of experimentation. In the dream, I was of the proper age for the procedure, and although I knew I wouldn't die from the surgery, the idea of a major organ being removed while I lay on the operating table gave me the terrifying and surreal feeling of being temporarily dead. This is how I felt about my son, being kept alive by machine. I just didn't want to know.

I think Mom was keenly aware of my additional stress this time around. She took care of her daughter the best way she knew how. "Do you feel like going to the gift shop? I think you need a present."

I was glad that she could tell I needed gifties—apparently I had that I-need-the-comfort-of-shopping look in my eyes, and Mom was more than happy to tend to that necessity. She walked me to the hospital gift shop, and after looking around for nearly 45 minutes to make just the right choice, I decided on a large, flowered tote-bag that I could use to haul my belongings back and forth between home and Beverly Hills. Never satisfied with getting me only one present, she also bought me a pair of fuzzy purple slippers so that I could pad around the NICU in comfort. Mom knows just how to make me feel all better.

Walter and I did leave the hospital briefly to walk to a nearby store and purchase a DVD. Stress was high that day, and the perfect movie to de-stress with seemed to me to be *Student Bodies*, one of my all-time favorite guilty-pleasure movies. I hadn't seen it in years, and I was very proud to show Walter this often-watched cult classic from my high-school days. It was just as I remembered: super silly, and a great way to take up some time. Walter and I shared a set of ear buds, leaned in to each other and held hands while watching Malvert, The Breather, and varied images of illogical silliness on my laptop. I felt sufficiently guiltily pleased.

Another long day of waiting finally passed, and we were called and informed that Phillip's operation was a success; we could see him. Like last time, the best medicine for him at the moment was lots of rest—he was heavily drugged and sleeping. I looked at him—once again bandaged and tubed—and gave him a gentle kiss good-night. We all turned and walked into the hallway to leave, and I, right on cue, recommenced crying. My clueless husband asked, deep concern in his voice, "What's wrong?!" I responded with cranky-wife sarcasm, "My son just had a major operation." But a warm, understanding female doctor came to me and assured, "We are going to take very good care of him. He needs to rest now—that's what is going to be best for him." Seeing me wipe away a post-operative tear, she added, "And you need some rest, too. So, go home with your family, have a relaxing evening, and come back in the morning." The doctor gave me a hug and a few more words of assurance, and, with a glance back at Phillip's sleeping form, Walter and I turned to walk, arms around each other's shoulders, down the hall and to the car.

When we went to GrandMinnie's house to retrieve Heidi, she was glad to have us to herself for the evening. We took her out to dinner at her favorite Jewish Deli to give her some matzo ball soup and the attention she deserved.

Since our previous stay at BHCH, the children's hospital had been moved and refurbished. There were many more comforts available this time around, such as decorated and peaceful waiting rooms and private quarters for patients. After the operation, Phillip's room in the NICU, although crowded with monitors, was private and roomy enough to accommodate a rocking chair for me to sleep on. A wooden rocker was not the most comfortable sleeping choice, but it was emotionally more comfortable than being in a different city, 45 miles from my ailing child.

So, at 6:00 AM, I woke up before Walter and Heidi and headed to Beverly Hills. When I arrived at his hospital crib, Phillip was already awake. Again, I couldn't hold him because of all the tubes and wires—he had two drainage tubes in his abdomen this time, as well as some wires that went into his chest to directly monitor his heart rate. Should Phillip go into sudden cardiac arrest, the wires would stimulate his heart to begin beating again, like miniature internal paddles. These wires were very delicate and needed to be kept perfectly still, so Phillip had to remain lying down on his back, immobile, as long as the wires were in place. And, of course, he had the traditional breathing tube in his esophagus. So, I had to satisfy my desire to comfort him by reaching across the bed and touching his hair and cheeks.

I looked forward to the removal of Phillip's breathing tube, as it would bring at least one aspect of relief to his many discomforts, and because he would then be able to have the comfort of a bottle of formula. When the doctor decided Phillip could breathe well enough on his own, I stepped out of the room during the procedure, and came back to be his savior with a warm, comforting bottle of milk. I couldn't hold him for the feeding, the delicate wires still monitoring his heart, but I leaned over the bed and put my face close to his, gazing into his eyes while he ate.

Several hours later, nurses looked at Phillip's drainage tube with concerned expressions and quiet exclamations of "Uh oh."

When I responded, "Uh oh?" one of the nurses gently explained, "The liquid in his drainage tube looks white and foamy. That means he's draining fat. We'll show the doctor, but that will probably mean Phillip won't be able to eat or drink anything else until some thin membranes inside him heal."

Apparently, this was something that commonly occurs. During the heart operation, a very delicate membrane that is easily damaged was nicked, causing fat to begin leaking along with the usual fluids that drain after this type of operation. The phenomenon was not dangerous, but in order to let the membrane heal, all foods would have to be withheld until the fluid drained free of fats. So, Phillip could not have his comforting bottles, let alone rice cereal or jarred baby food, and he would need to get the okay from a doctor to even have water.

Very soon, Phillip was ready for something more substantial to eat than just a bottle of milk, and he made his desires known. The nurse let me give Phillip a pacifier dipped in sugar water. Each time I dipped the binky and presented it to my hungry child, he would suck enthusiastically until he realized no actual food was being administered, and he'd start to cry again. Eventually, he wouldn't accept the essence-of-sugar ruse at all, and he just cried. Soon, his wails of hunger were closer together with fewer and fewer pauses, until he screamed continuously, barely stopping for breath, for a solid four hours. Helpless, with no way to comfort my boy as time passed, I only stood at his bedside stroking his hair and kissing his cheek until the nurse returned with an okay from the doctor to give Phillip Pedialite. The nurse brought in several jars of the hydrating, clear liquid, and even though it was basically the equivalent of water, when I attached a nipple to the container and presented it to Phillip, he drank it with the enthusiasm of a wanderer lost for weeks in the Sahara. Instantly, the fluid was drained from the bottle, and just as instantly, Phillip fell asleep. Exhausted from so many hours of hungry crying, my tired baby slept through the night for the first time in his tiny life, a full 14 hours. I was grateful for the monitors and alarms that kept track of his heart rate and respiration because, amidst his sleepy silence, I occasionally worried that he had expired from the exhaustion of so many hours spent wailing for food. But his silence had simply manifested from his respite from hunger, and he was sleeping as he should have—like a baby. With a sigh of relief, I fell asleep in the rocking chair at his bedside. In the middle of the night, I awoke to find myself covered with a blanket, Phillip still sleeping peacefully.

* * *

When Phillip's heartbeats had proven themselves to be regular and strong, the internal wires could be removed from his chest. The removal was an extremely delicate procedure; the doctor had to perform the extrication painfully slowly, pulling the wires out a nanometer at a time, keeping a close eye on a special monitor between each short pull. Phillip had to lie perfectly still during removal, so Mom held Phillip's arms down until he quietly began to weep. Our cuddly boy had been longing to be held in someone's loving arms for days now. After several agonizing minutes, as soon as the wires were pulled completely free, the nurse asked Mom to pull Phillip up into a sitting position so his remaining cords and tubes could be realigned. Upright, Phillip threw his arms around his Grammy, comforting himself in her warm embrace after an uncomfortable procedure and days without cuddles. Grammy willingly obliged and the two shared a long, reassuring hug—probably quite soothing for not only Phillip but Grammy as well, knowing that she was so desperately necessary as a conduit for reassurance. We quickly prepared a rocking chair and pillow and organized the drainage tubes and remaining wires so I could hold my baby in my lap—I wanted to share in the comfort-giving as well.

After a few more days in the NICU, we were allowed to move to a regular room. This was another private room with a recliner next to his crib, but with the accommodating addition of a fold-out couch under the large window opening onto a view of Beverly Hills. And the room had a private bathroom. We didn't have a shower, but the easy ability to freshen up felt luxurious. We brought in a few personal items from home to brighten up Phillip's room. The Edith-Mobile was a necessity, and I printed 5"x7" photographs of sister, parents, grandparents, and favorite cousins Ashley, Shawn and Vanessa to tape up on the clear plastic canopy that draped over the top of the crib and down the head and foot. Phillip spent a lot of time looking at the pictures and naming his relatives, especially his buddy, Papa; that photo was second in favor only to Rob's in-person visits.

I was glad for Phillip's comforting bottles of Pedialite, for he wasn't allowed to eat or drink anything else for four more days. On the fifth day of a solid Pedialite-only diet, when the draining fluids were clear of fat, we were finally allowed to give him a welcome bottle of formula. To assure that Phillip's nicked membrane could heal fully, his diet would have to remain fat-free for six weeks. He was given a special baby formula that conformed to his new diet, and he drank it down with delight. Within minutes, he responded to the tasty meal with explosive diarrhea and projectile vomiting. I held him in place, impeding his desire to wriggle around in newly-present bodily expulsions, while Mom calmly and repeatedly pressed the nurse's call button. Apparently, Phillip was partial, and physically accustomed, to his formula from home. The nurses promptly ordered a fat-free equivalent formula which was later delivered in a large case to Phillip's room. In the meantime, the nurse removed all of Phillip's bedding and gave him a sponge bath. He promptly forgot the recent formula propulsion and enjoyed playing with the nurse's bucket of soapy water.

A few days passed with Phillip's chest wounds continuing to heal well. He was certainly sore, but he did seem to find solace in being held. I would generally hold him in my lap throughout the night, as I had done during his previous hospitalization, the nurse changing his diaper by flashlight right there in my arms.

After about six days, Phillip's drainage tubes could be removed. During the removal process, Mom and I sat on the couch under the window, allowing the doctor and nurse to work freely. This time, I was much less wary of the tube removal procedure; I knew he would be temporarily uncomfortable, but I also knew he would be much more comfortable immediately afterward. He had two such tubes this time, both about a centimeter in diameter, so their removal was surely as unpleasant as before, and the entrance wounds had to be stitched closed. Being near his navel, the two additional holes made his tummy look like there were three belly buttons.

The tubes were apparently much more undesirable than we thought; as soon as both of them were gone, Phillip wanted to sit up on his own. Later that evening, he grasped the railings of his hospital crib to stand and get close-up views of the family pictures at the foot of the bed.

The familiar hospital volunteer came by with a cart of books and toys, and Phillip was presented with a *Corduroy* book and a matching teddy bear, which he looked at and talked to for hours. This was the first time we ever saw him take interest in a stuffed animal, and we celebrated this new development by purchasing additional cuddly toys from the gift shop. Once again, his completed surgery was providing him with the additional strength necessary to develop further, and he began immediately to exhibit huge jumps in physical and conceptual development. He smiled at Corduroy, turned pages in the book, rocked back and forth to music from a supplied CD player, pointed at pictures of Papa, and charmed the nurses with his flirty looks, shy smiles and breathy chuckles.

With my baby feeling and looking so much healthier and happier, I began really enjoying my time with Phillip in the hospital. We would spend many hours chatting, giggling, singing, listening to CDs, and cuddling in the crib-side reclining chair.

On one particularly relaxing day, while snuggling and watching television together in the armchair of Phillip's sixth-floor room, I felt a sudden jostling of the recliner. When I looked up from Phillip's big blue eyes, I saw his IV begin to sway, and I heard that sound which is so familiar to a Southern California native—rumbling ceiling, floor and walls caused by an earthquake. This was my first time being up so high during a tremor, and as the building was so new and so modernly designed to withstand a quake, I felt immensely safe. From the motion of the building, I could tell very clearly that it had been built on rollers of some sort. The building moved like a floating cruise ship on calm seas. For several minutes after the tectonic plates had settled back into place, the building continued to roll gently back and forth like an eight-story hammock swaying in the southern California Pacific breeze. Nurses quickly went into each room to ensure that patients and visitors were unharmed and felt safe, but my boy and I didn't require consolation. I looked at Phillip and said, like a true Californian, "That was kind of fun." He looked back and smiled; I'm sure he agreed.

Mom, whenever possible, liked to spend time with Phillip in our room. She would tend to her grandmotherly desires of spoiling and playing while allowing me a few minutes to go down to the cafeteria or to take a nap on the provided couch. During one of her visits, while she sat on the couch looking through the mail she had brought from my house to organize, and while I rested in the recliner holding Phillip, several doctors—five or six at least—filed into our room and stood around Phillip and me in a semi-circle. I was used to one doctor's visit at a time, several times throughout the day. But there were numerous doctors with us now, some whom I didn't recognize. The way they stood around Phillip and me like the mezzanine of a theater, I thought maybe they were expecting us to break into a rendition of "Putting on the Ritz" for their entertainment. Before getting too concerned by their audience-like presence, I observed their expressions—they were all smiling.

Following traditional greetings, one doctor finally presented the vital question, "How would you like to bring your son home today?"

The comforts of the hospital were a great improvement over our previous visit, but being in a hospital never measures up to being at home. So, my immediate response to the doctor's inquiry was, "I love you all dearly, but—woo hoo!" The doctors smiled with understanding.

We were instructed to pack up our belongings and be ready to leave the hospital at 11:00 AM, and I was more than thrilled to comply. I called Walter at work and told him to take the rest of the day off to come to BHCH and help us load the car and get us home.

Even after this relatively short hospital stay—six days—we repacked as if we had been on vacation for a month, bringing home much more than we had arrived with. Walter, Mom and I originally brought our basic belongings, but with each nightly trip home and morning return visit, we would bring additional supplies, realizing that we could have used another pillow or book. Additionally, we were packing up and going home with numerous jars and cans of Phillip's still-required fat-free baby formula and the necessary bottles and nipples, along with the much-appreciated hospital-provided diapers and wipes. And this time, we learned to take absolutely everything that BHCH gifted to us. So, we also brought home bulb syringes, bandages, alcohol wipes, tape removal fluid, gauze pads, and any other item that we had been given and subsequently would be billed for, any member of our household might or might not eventually need, and the hospital would only dispose of. Most importantly, we also had the plentiful donated toys that had been given to Phillip by joyful volunteers, along with several gifts from family and friends who had visited during Phillip's stay. We were well stocked on many aspects of daily living. In all, we packed up about five garbage bags full of things to lug home.

After completing the traditional dummy check of every drawer and cabinet, Mom and I sat with Phillip, anxiously awaiting 11:00, watching every movement of the clock's hands, willing them to rush forward to the hour when we had been approved to finally go home.

Each time a nurse would come in to check on Phillip's wellbeing, we would say, "He's doing great—he gets to go home at 11:00!" When the sweet young volunteer came in with her cart, asking her usual, "Would your baby like any books or toys?" I beamed and announced, "He doesn't need any more toys—he's going home at 11:00!" With a bright smile, she congratulated us, said goodbye to Phillip, and gave him a book to take home.

With our bags lined up on the couch and ready to go, as soon as the clock's minute hand clicked into place, 11:00 to the second, Mom and I rapidly removed electrode stickers from Phillip's chest (gently, of course) and pulled off the remaining external wires and monitors. We gave Phillip one last diaper change before Walter showed up and began lugging bags and belongings out to the car.

Then, a nurse came in. "I saw at the nurse's station that Phillip's monitors are disconnected. Maybe they jostled loose or something. Can I check them?"

I happily explained to her, "We're leaving at 11:00. We took the wires off."

"Oh," replied the befuddled nurse. Apparently, that wasn't quite what we were meant to do. "I have to make one last check of his vitals before he can be released. 11:00 is the time to check out, but we have to go through some procedures first."

I felt a bit silly. As the nurse tried to do her last checking and logging with all of Phillip's equipment removed, I realized that, not being a nurse myself, I may have wanted to wait and take the final getting-the-heck-out-of-the-hospital steps in the presence of someone who actually knew what they were doing. What a dope.

But soon enough, the knowledgeable RN finished what she needed to do, gave Phillip a final good-bye, and sent us on our way. I carried my boy in my arms this time, rather than in his car seat, and we waved to everyone as we walked past the nurse's station, through the hallways, and to the valet parking lot.

* * *

For both operations, Dr. McMann had had to cut through Phillip's breast bone. When the bones healed, they formed a pointed V shape, like a miniature Mt. Fuji poking out of the center of Phillip's chest. The bump bothered some people who felt or saw it, and Mom often asked me if I thought it was getting bigger. I didn't, but on Mom's behalf I asked Dr. Singh about it. He told me Phillip was quite lucky, as some post-operative breastbones actually heal with an inward curve. Phillip's outward protrusion acted as a protective barrier to his heart that would keep him safe from jolts and knocks. And it certainly wasn't growing—it looked just right, Dr. Singh assured, and was appropriate for what the surgeon had put it through.

Still, people commented on it. If anyone held Phillip and felt the bump, they'd ask me about it with concern. Some people thought it was a therapeutic device strapped to the front of his chest. But it's just part of Phillip's anatomy now. Phillip's Uncle Keith lovingly refers to "Bump Boy" at least once per visit.

As Phillip grows, the bump seems to be receding. But whether or not it goes away or remains, we don't mind. It is a post-operative trophy which we will teach Phillip to own with pride.

Chapter 23:

Completion

With the drama surrounding two heart surgeries, the busy bustle of several-times-weekly therapies, as well as a daughter with hours of homework daily (hours due to the as yet undiagnosed ADHD—but that's the next book), and numerous after-school activities, Walter and I realized that it had been quite a while and we had heard nothing about the completion of Phillip's adoption. He was nearing his third birthday, but was actually still not "ours" on paper. We, therefore, made a call to the social worker, but she was unreachable—on maternity leave—and no one else seemed to be in charge of our case. A couple of additional calls with no gained headway led us to decide that we needed to take a next proactive step.

A neighbor referred us to an adoption attorney in the area of our hometown. Our new, more local adoption lawyer, Melissa, was a gift from the gods of bureaucracy-battling. After a meeting with her and a few phone calls, she found where our paperwork had been misplaced. Melissa discovered that, apparently, the attorney in San Francisco, Pauline, seemed to have dropped the ball—she should have contacted us months ago to complete the legal portion of the adoption process. I'm sure Pauline was merely backlogged, but, as nice as she was, I was more than willing to take one of her case burdens away from her. I wanted this adoption completed.

Two weeks after finding Melissa, she secured an appointment at the courthouse for the finalization of the adoption—on Phillip's third birthday.

For the past five years, we had been through so many stressful and heartbreaking moments—two years of home study and three years of adoption—that when the court date approached, I began to worry. Was this actually going to happen, or would it be another adoption disappointment? To add to my worry, I had never spoken to a judge other than during jury duty, and, so far, adoption had been an extreme strain on my self-esteem and emotional strength. As Phillip's birthday approached, I fretted, "What will the judge ask us? What will she think of us?"

As much as possible, I tried to set aside negative thoughts and focus on the finalization of this lengthy venture; no matter what anyone at West Coast might have said in the past, I tried to convince myself that Walter and I really were good parents, and the judge would only be asking us questions we could confidently answer.

Walter gathered up a tie and dress-shoes, and I donned my best outfit. Grammy gifted Heidi with a brand new, elegant black dress. But Phillip, the star of the show, wore black pants, a white dress-shirt, and a brown-and-gold paisley vest with matching bowtie. His outfit would make him look handsome and classy, and I was looking forward to flaunting him with parental pride.

Melissa had previously told me that we could bring family to the courthouse, as well as someone to take pictures. Having been given that permission, I planned to have the courtroom packed with Phillip's greatest and most important fans: Grammy, Papa, Grandpa, Grandma, and GrandMinnie. Next to what the judge would think of us and ask us, my biggest concern was capturing sufficient photographs of the event. To assure proper documentation of the occasion, I invited three of my closest friends. My ex-coworker and awesomely good friend, Denise, and my friend with the couch for between-hospital-visit crashing, Sam, would both take videos; and Sam's wife, Atusa, would take pictures.

Then, it happened. A glitch.

The day before the court appointment to meet with a big scary judge and be approved or turned down for the completion of the adoption, Phillip was playing out in the front yard when he ran, tripped on a crack in the sidewalk, fell flat on his face, and gouged out a huge chunk of skin from the end of his tiny nose. On adoption day, while handsomely clad, he would arrive at the courthouse with a quarter-sized bloody scab in the center of his face. I was already worried about what the judge might think of us as parents, but now we would look like abusers. Terrific.

The situation reminded me of our final interview with the social worker in Whittier. The day before that interview, Heidi had chosen that moment to give Phillip's cheek a big, scarlet hickey. Right in the middle of his cheek. A hickey. Thankfully, when I explained the cause of the bright red blotch, the social worker merely laughed and noted, "Well, obviously she loves her brother!" I prayed the judge would be as forgiving.

On the morning of June 14, our happy group—parents, sister, grandparents, and friendly paparazzi—gathered at the Pine Valley Court House. Although nervous, I was excited and hopeful that I might be seeing this rocky, uneven, uphill path to adoption come to an end. My dad signed us in, and we all sat on the benches which lined the hallway, anticipating our turn with the judge.

After a very short wait, we could see, bobbing over the tops of the entrance's walk-through metal detectors, a large bundle of balloons, one with the appropriate message, "Happy Birthday!" Sure enough, around the corner came our attorney, Melissa. She met us with congratulatory hugs, handed the balloons to Phillip, and took our pictures. Seeing her joyous, light-hearted behavior allowed my nerves to relax significantly.

With Melissa's arrival, we were immediately called into the courtroom. Inside the chambers were a judge, a court reporter, and a bailiff. The judge was a tall, slim young woman with a teddy-bear-brown pageboy haircut and fashionable, thick-rimmed glasses over her welcoming green eyes and smiling cheeks. She wore the traditional judge's robe, but she was sitting in front of a small table in the center of the room, rather than behind her large, official, scary judge's bench. On that particular podium, rather than a judge, sat 20 or 30 stuffed animals of various types surrounding a large white plastic bowl of lollipops.

The judge greeted us with smiles and handshakes, and asked us to sit around the small table, Walter and I across from her, Heidi standing next to Walter, and Phillip sitting on my lap. The grandparents and lawyer sat in chairs behind the semicircular table which curved around the perimeter of the room. Atusa, Denise, and Sam, standing in scattered locations about the room, began snapping and recording.

My nerves had relaxed, but they disappeared completely when the judge began her legal proceedings. I had expected today's line of questions to be difficult ones, like those Eliza had asked us years ago. But, not only did the judge not have those questions for us, she didn't ask us one single question. She didn't even ask what we had irresponsibly done to Phillip's nose.

After presenting Walter and me with one or two forms to sign, the judge announced, "Now, when I sign this form, Phillip will become your son with all the rights and responsibilities of a natural-born child."

Natural-born child. Not even our adopted child. Our natural-born child. That struck me profoundly.

Years of trial and heartache were coming to a conclusion with the simple swipe of a pen. Phillip had always been ours, but I had a lingering worry that he could be, somehow, taken from us because he wasn't ours on paper. But in a moment, as I began to hear the judge say those words that I had waited so long to hear—even better than what I had imagined hearing—our natural-born child—we would be safe from any future concern of having our baby's relation to us denied.

"This child is now the adopted child of the petitioners, Walter and Sarah-Jane Cavilry, and shall be in the custody of said petitioners and regarded and treated in all respects as their lawful child; that they shall sustain toward the child and the child toward them the legal relationship of parents and child, and each respectfully shall have all of the rights and be subject to all of the duties of natural parent and child; and that the name of said child shall henceforth be Jonathon Phillip Cavilry."

And the judge signed her name. She then presented Walter and me with a colorful certificate commemorating the day, permitted Phillip to choose a teddy bear, and asked Heidi to pass out lollipops.

That was it. No questions. No moral judgment. No telling us what she really thought of our personalities or motivations. Just a couple of signatures and we were done. He was ours. Phillip was ours.

I held my boy—my Phillip—as we walked out of the courthouse. Everywhere we went for the rest of the day—restaurant, park, grocery store—I held Phillip proudly, announcing to friends and strangers alike, "We just adopted him today. We've had him since he was four days old, but his adoption was final today. He's officially ours."

The world was bright, the future shiny and new in front of us.
The Cavilry family was complete.

Chapter 24:
Celebration

Two days after our visit to the courthouse, on a bright summer afternoon, we rejoiced. The wait for this conclusion had been long—years long—and we celebrated at our deserved level of extravagance.

Mom organized and hosted a catered party in the park for 40 of our relatives and friends. The festivities were complete with five varieties of gourmet sandwiches, three types of accompanying salads, full-size carnival-style snow cone and popcorn machines, and an enormous red and blue inflatable jumper. Seeing the warm sun shining on our comfortably breezy day, my joyous, grinning loved ones, and my baby boy, I could barely contain my desire to get into the jumper and bounce around with celebratory glee. Walter didn't contain his desire—he got right in and bounced.

After everyone had enjoyed sandwiches, salads, and a snow cone or two, I gathered up the guests for a little speech. I asked my friend, Amber, a fellow sign language interpreter, to come up and interpret so that Atusa and Sam, who are deaf, could understand what was being said.

I was barely able to mutter, "Everyone, I'd like to make an announcement…" before I began to cry. Not just cry, but to sob. Heaving, wet, uncontrollable sobs. All the stress and tension of the last several years, combined with the presence and security of the people I love most, burst through at that moment in waves of grateful, involuntary release. My scrunched-up, purple, sopping, snotty face was mortifyingly embarrassing, but I didn't give up. I had things to say and I was going to say them.

"I've always had an emotional connection with people with disabilities, especially Down syndrome."

Phillip came to me and asked to be held, then whined and asked to be put down. After a few more sounds of protest, I showed him the tears streaming down my cheeks and said, "Look at me, honey, this is important." The guests gave a little laugh, Atusa tried to take Phillip to the jumper, and we finally decided he just wanted to sit with Daddy, which he did.

I continued, "A lot of people have helped me with this whole life-changing thing, adopting this baby. I want to thank some people. But first…"

I grabbed some tissue, provided by Mom—of course—mopped up my liquidy face, and continued.

"This all came to a conclusion on Friday when we finally adopted him. So, we completed the adoption. He's not Caden Michael Greene anymore. He's our Cavilry baby." That brought out a cheer from the crowd and provoked me to perform the classy and feminine fist pump.

With a few tears in her big blue eyes but a smile on her face, Heidi said, "You're crying, and now I'm gonna start crying very soon."

"You're already crying," was my teasing response. She gave me a loving look and the will to continue. Taking a deep breath, I began again.

"There are several people who I want to say thank you for what they've done in helping with this whole thing. And, really, because a lot of people have asked me, 'Why Down syndrome? Why do you want to do this?' But throughout whatever questions, they've still just completely taken him into their hearts and really welcomed him into the family, and I appreciate that.

"So I have some awards for people."

I reached below the table in front of me and pulled up a large box full of framed awards. That elicited a very sweet, "Aww," from the crowd. Sniveling but stubbornly plugging away, I presented certificates of appreciation to some very deserving key individuals who needed to be recognized, although thanking them adequately was impossible: Tess from down the street who gives Phillip Doritos whenever he insists on some; his cousin, my brother's son, who comes out for weekend visits and asks to hold his little cousin; interpreter friends Denise and Naomi who stood by me and gave me hugs when I needed them. Mini Anna was unavailable to attend, but was certainly worthy of an award.

Next, six more awards were given to key accepting, grateful, vital family members.

"For, regardless of any initial personal concerns, setting those worries aside and, not only accepting our beloved Phillip Cavilry into your family, but taking him lovingly and permanently into your heart."

Mom, my dad and step-mom, and Walter's mom were called up for teary hugs and to receive their awards. Rob—Papa—had been intentionally skipped over. I have often wondered if he felt unappreciated at that moment. But then I presented the next award.

"For, unquestioningly, taking Phillip Cavilry into your family, home, and heart; for committing yourself to his care, wellbeing, growth, and development; and for being the loving, devoted role-model whom Phillip will remember and cherish his entire life—Papa."

When I said his name, he slowly lifted each extreme-sport-scarred leg over the picnic bench where he sat and sauntered up, face expressionless, but when we hugged, I heard his muffled sobs. I knew he was a very proud grandfather.

Then came the two most vital awards, given to the people who I couldn't have embarked upon this adventure without.

With a pale pine frame, lovingly hand-decorated (by her mommy) with vines, flowers, and hearts, the second-to-last certificate read, "For being the most loving, caring, protective, educational, devoted, entertaining, talented, and beautiful big sister that we could ever wish to have for our son...Heidi."

Heidi came up and proudly accepted her award. She put aside her bubbly, energetic, talkative side for a moment and walked up to me for a quiet, serious hug. I think she was sharing some of the relief from worry that I was experiencing that day. For years, she had been put through the stress of my stress, but had gone on to love her brother anyway; at eight years old, she was Phillip's best friend and greatest supporter. Her brother is a lucky guy.

Last came the most important award of all. As I forced myself to read through my tears, I heard unmuffled sobs from the group, and my tough-guy brother-in-law, Keith, put on his sunglasses to, I know, hide his moistening eyes.

I recited, "For, so readily, joining me on this miraculous adventure by, not only accepting a new little baby boy into our family, but by committing yourself to the long and arduous adoption process; by devoting yourself to being the best father that you can be; by faithfully continuing to do whatever is necessary for his physical and mental development; by being exceedingly proud of your son's genius and accomplishments; and for loving our little Phillip with all of your heart and soul. Walter, I love you more than words can express. I couldn't ask for a better father for my children."

The words of the last two sentences could barely make their way out of my constricted, failing vocal chords, but I pushed through; no matter how drenched in tears my face might be or how ridiculous my voice might sound while I sniffled and snorted, those were the most important sentences of the day, and I wanted to say those words out loud and in public.

We had walked up such a difficult road, but Walter had remained right by my side through the entire journey. And he didn't just support my decision to adopt; he worked hard to make the concept a reality and become a devoted daddy, Phillip's favorite person in the world. Phillip is Daddy's Boy through and through, and Walter welcomes and cherishes that title with honor.

Much later on, I found out that I had been very rude to someone at the party. With no preparation and no professional reimbursement, I had asked Amber to come up and interpret for me, and when I started reading Walter's award and bawling, I made Amber cry, too. I felt bad when I found out that I had not only put her on the spot professionally but emotionally.

But I also felt kind of good that what I said had touched her heart, along with the hearts of many other guests, judging by the sound of the sobbing coming from the crowd.

Lastly, I said the one phrase that I had been mentally rehearsing, repeating over and over to myself for months, if not years. Now, I could finally verbalize the sentence, the words that meant we had truly reached the end of our journey.

"Let's, please, welcome Phillip Cavilry into our family."

Over the years, I've often found that the responses of others to my comments or actions is not always—usually is not—what I act out in my mental fantasies. I might imagine that, if I say or do such-and-such, so-and-so will laugh or be amused or react with interest. But when the time comes and I say what I've planned, so-and-so's reaction doesn't conform to my preconceived fantasy. Like an audience member beginning a slow clap only to end up standing and cheering alone in a crowd of open-mouthed onlookers.

But on the occasion of Phillip's adoption party, all of my fantasies played out in precise duplication to my mental images, maybe a little better than I had imagined. The award certificates were a very important message for me to convey, and the message was accepted with serious reverence and gratitude. But, most importantly, when I announced those long-fantasized lines, "...welcome Phillip Cavilry into our family," my audience—Phillip's fans—cheered and clapped to put all of my fantasies to shame. Their verbose explosion of love and acceptance brightened my eyes more than the concluding firework finale on the fourth of July. More than any other on that joyous day, I will remember that moment forever.

Then all of Phillip's guests, family, friends, jubilant party-goers, stood for hugs, more tears, and some words of love for Phillip. We passed around cake decorated with primary colors and ABC blocks beginning the joyful words, "Adoption Birthday Celebration." Guests showered Phillip with gifts of his favorite items: a king-sized bag of Doritos, a ball decorated with pictures of SpongeBob, a Toy Story's Rex-shaped flashlight, and, his most treasured gift, a push-broom from Uncle Keith. My son sat in the center of the picnic table, surrounded by his gifts, his devoted followers sitting and looking up at him like townspeople viewing an honored king from his balcony. Phillip was encouraged to play with and admire each offering before opening each succeeding present, his mouth unapologetically smeared with Doritos' cheese powder and chocolate cake.

He was king for a day, and rightfully so.

Chapter 25:

Phillip

Over the past three years, what has Phillip been like? Is he different from what uninformed people might think of a child with Down syndrome? Is he like children who don't have Down syndrome? Many people have told me, "I could never do what you did," or, "You are an angel for adopting him." Considering what he was when he was born and what he is now, what is it about him that makes people who don't know him think they wouldn't be able to raise someone like him?

Here is what I have observed regarding Phillip—the behavior that makes him "different".

Before he could sit up, he would lie on his stomach and repeatedly straighten his legs and thrust his arms forward, posing like Superman flying through the clouds.

He never did crawl properly, choosing instead an army-style tummy-to-the-ground low creep, then later a rapid ambulation on his bottom, swinging himself forward with left arm and right leg, left leg tucked away—his "monkey crawl".

When he finally walked at age two, he did so with an unending devotion, falling and getting back up enthusiastically, laughing uncontrollably at our wildly supportive cheers and applause.

At three years old, toddling with steady confidence, he now walks around the checkout stands at the grocery store and high-fives everyone in line.

If he does something naughty, like throwing something in the house, we ask, "Do you want to go to your room?" to which he shouts, "No, Keith!" meaning, quite logically, "No, thank you very much, I'd rather go visit Uncle Keith."

Whenever possible, he orders each person in a room to stand and dance, with or without music. An unplanned dance party always ensues.

If he sees a gray-haired grandmotherly-type in a restaurant or store, he'll unfailingly go up and give her a hug.

Phillip is different. But none of his difference has anything to do with Down syndrome; it just has to do with him being Phillip. There is no child in the world like him. His adorableness, his sweetness, his humor—his difference—is what makes him amazing, and it's what makes me want to proudly show him off, to make everyone see, like any proud mom, that I have the best son in the world. Phillip happens to have Down syndrome, but this condition is such a small part of what makes him unique, I almost want to avoid mentioning it here. However, it's part of him, and I'm proud of every part.

People have had, almost solely, positive reactions toward Phillip. When we walk around in public with him, we commonly and continuously get toothy grins and wide-eyed *awws* from strangers, often along with comments on his contagious cuteness or gorgeous red hair. But most often, he just gets silent smiles of human appreciation. On walks around the block, neighbors will often greet him by name: "Hey, Phillip! Where you going, Buddy?" At the grocery store, we have to visit each of the checkers, who then argue over who gets to check him through at their register (and then, unfailingly, we have to wait through a new series of high-fives all around.)

Phillip is loved wherever he goes. Even when kids at Heidi's school see Phillip, they come up to him to comment on how cute he is, or they stand back and tell their friends, "Look at the baby. He is so cute!" When we drop Heidi off at her best friend Allie's house for a sleepover, before Heidi goes inside, Allie runs out to poke her head through the car window and give Phillip a hug.

I have great hope for Phillip's future happiness.

I had briefly been concerned that Phillip wouldn't be accepted by our friends and relatives. Although rarely, Walter and I have heard negative, worried comments from the people in regard to Phillip's Down syndrome. One of my closest friends told me, "I could never do that. If I was pregnant and found out my baby had Down syndrome, I'd have an abortion." Of course, even when life seems perfect, there are exceptions like those. Luckily, the exceptions have been few, and we have been learning to deal with them with a positive attitude and understanding.

After we brought Phillip into our home, Heidi became very attracted to the idea of Down syndrome, gleefully announcing, "There's a Down syndrome!" whenever she saw a person of that particular variety on the street or in a store. She was very disappointed to find out that, when she was born, she had not been a baby with Down syndrome like her little brother.

When the two of us were lollygagging down the sidewalk, slowly working our way to her kindergarten classroom, Heidi saw a young mother pushing a baby in a stroller and asked, hopefully, "Excuse me, is she a Down syndrome?" I quickly explained to the obviously confused mother, "Her little brother has Down syndrome, so she thinks all babies might." The mother softly replied with an apologetic sorrow in her voice, "Well, strange things happen."

I was taken aback momentarily when I realized, "She thinks I gave birth to a baby with Down syndrome—and that it's *bad*." Not certain how to respond, but wanting to say something to enlighten her, I inadvertently spurted, "Oh, we adopted him!" That didn't explain much. What I really wanted to add was, "We are *glad* he has Down syndrome—that's what we wanted!" I felt a need to stick up for my son—his birth was not something about which I needed to be consoled, and I actually resented her for having done so.

My father has always taught me to believe the best in people. If a person makes a comment which comes out sounding unappealing, their words are generally not intended with negativity or malice. The recipient of the comment is the one who has the choice to hear the words positively or negatively. And I know he's right, just as I know that woman wasn't being evil. She merely didn't know what to say, and felt that she needed to say *something*. So, she said what she felt most appropriate, suddenly finding herself in the awkward position of having to say something to a mother who had given birth to a disabled baby. But at hearing her reaction to my son, my motherly instincts kicked in. I didn't want Phillip's existence to be an occasion for sympathy, for saying to oneself, "Oh geez, how do I respond to her tragedy?" and then giving a comforting comment during my time of trial. And, although I remember what Dad always said—you can take things negatively or positively—every time I see that woman at my daughter's school, I think, "That's the woman who, had Phillip been hers, would have been upset."

My logic and emotions are often in conflict. I always try to be a good role-model on the outside, but as a real-life mom of a child with Down syndrome, my inner thoughts sometimes betray what might be considered "right."

Several times during the adoption process, from people close to the Down syndrome community as well as laymen, I was told that raising a child with Down syndrome is an undertaking that some parents simply don't feel capable of handling. Therefore, those unable parents might decide to give their child up for adoption, and that is an acceptable and understandable conclusion.

Over the years, I have tried very hard to understand and accept that stance, as it seems to be the opinion held by Down syndrome advocates and, therefore, the stance I should take as well.

However, after trying repeatedly to be politically correct, I just have to admit—I have a very difficult time embracing that viewpoint. I've tried to be compassionate, but my brain continues to refuse to comprehend how a parent can create a baby and give the little guy away.

This opinion is coming from a woman who took one of those given-away babies. Phillip's birth mother gave us the greatest gift imaginable. She completed our family. I owe my familial wholeness to her, and I am grateful, every day for the decisions she made. And I have no idea how she could have done it.

When she gave up her baby, as Betsy told me, a friend of Loretta's vowed never to speak to her again; the friend's own sister had Down syndrome. A pregnant colleague of mine told me that if her currently gestating fetus tested positive on an upcoming screening for Down syndrome, she was planning to abort; I knew, if she aborted, I would never be able to speak to her again. Her abortion would have meant a vicarious rejection of my son. But I am forever indebted and grateful for the decision made my one of those very rejecters.

I'm completely aware that my opinions are contradictory, and I'm slowly coming to accept that as an unavoidable paradox. I must keep in the forefront of my mind the fact that, although I believe she *should* have kept him, if Loretta *had* kept Phillip, my family would now be without the greatest gift of our lives.

Still, my brain hurts every time I think of a mother giving away her child.

When parents expect a baby, the future mom and dad will undoubtedly have curious anticipatory musings about what their new baby will be like. "Maybe his hair will be curly like mine." "Will she have Mommy's nose?" "I hope he's musical like Grandpa." The prospective parents may even have fleeting conversations about what they don't want. "I want a boy, not a girl," or even, "It would be horrible to have an ugly baby," But it seems to me that parents generally love their babies, no matter what they end up with, even to the extent that the occasional ugly little tyke appears beautiful in mother's loving eye.

The possibilities for various types of children are even vaster than what is typically anticipated. A child may grow to be a scientific genius, finding a cure for cancer, or may grow to be extremely mediocre in professional pursuits, never holding more than minimum-wage employment. Should a parent love the over-achieving child more than the under, or feel an ability or inability to raise one type of child over the other? If traits like future strengths and weaknesses were detectable in the womb, would the minimum-wage earner's life be terminated? Or would he be given up for adoption? Or what about a plain child versus a beautiful one? Or gay versus straight? Or perfect pitch versus tone deaf? Or earless, eyeless, armless, or legless? Of all the possible combinations of genes and types of resulting offspring, why not allow a wider range of acceptable outcomes? Blonde and blue-eyed? That's the baby you made. Harelip and Tourette syndrome? That's the baby you made. No legs and stomach on the outside of its body? That's the baby you made. Profoundly developmentally disabled? That's the baby you made. Strengths, weaknesses, or just simple "variety," you made it. Take the child you personally created and expand your mind. Learn something new. Have a new experience. Begin an adventure. If the child you created grows to say a tearful, loving good-bye to you at your death bed, be thankful for every step of the path that brought him to your side. If the little baby you give birth to is only expected to live for an hour, let him spend that hour in his mother's arms.

The available combinations of genes and imaginable mutations of offspring are limitless, and in this game of random combinations called childbirth, we end up with a kid. How about if we love the kid we end up with? It's variety that makes life colorful and vibrant. Why not expand the rainbow? There are more possibilities than just the commonly accepted ROY G. BIV. There's scarlet, ruby, chartreuse, burgundy, rose, crimson, and then on to orange. If all of those colors were welcomed, the rainbow would be way more beautiful and exponentially more interesting.

The loving parent of any typical, non-disabled child would surely affirm, "I would do anything for my baby." That parent would, if needed, donate a kidney if it meant a longer life for their child. Why does Down syndrome not deserve the same I'd-do-anything assertion?

What is it about the gene combination resulting in Down syndrome that makes a child unwanted? I might not be able to see it, but it's apparently there. As I said, I've been told, more than once, "I could never do what you're doing," and "You're angels for adopting him," and the rare, "I would have done the same thing as the birth mother." What is it about Down syndrome that makes a child unlovable?

I'm sure that raising Phillip is going to be hard, and there have already been challenges, but there have been challenges raising Heidi as well. When she was four, at daycare, she hit a kid on the head with a wooden toy hammer, leaving a golf-ball sized lump above his eyebrow. In kindergarten, Heidi would sneak small toys into her pockets and bring them home. She's said the f-word in front of my mom more than once. And I can't get her to stop picking her effing nose. But, we have worked hard and made it through every single challenge, and, boogers and all, I wouldn't trade that girl for all the money in the world. And the same goes for Phillip. He knocks over the dog food and kicks the pieces of kibble around the kitchen. He refuses to sit on a potty. He screams if I brush his hair. He whines incessantly whenever we drive in the car. But there's nothing in his being which would make me ever consider wanting to be in the world without him in it.

Yes, Phillip has delays. At his age, when other kids are stringing together three- and four-word sentences, Phillip is only verbalizing one or two syllables at a time. He is nowhere near ready to transition out of diapers. But his delays also bring his babyness; I hold him in my arms and cuddle him and am thankful that I can enjoy his childhood a little longer than the typical quickly-developing toddler.

I've heard, probably, all of my mother-friends say, at least once, "My baby is growing up so fast." Well, my baby is growing up a little more slowly. I get to keep him younger for longer. I get to rock him to sleep and kiss him and cuddle him for several additional, precious years. I'm blessed by his delays; they mean, while Heidi is growing and becoming independent, I can still selfishly hang on to one of my babies a little longer.

He did have the challenge of two open-heart surgeries. Seeing my baby in that much pain, going through that much recovery, was a horrible experience that I would never wish on any parent or child. But I stayed by his side every minute, just as I would have if it were Heidi.

Suppose a child, at the age of five, developed leukemia. Should a parent always be expected to say, "I'll do anything for my child"? Would it be acceptable for some parents to say, "I'm just not able to take this on," and give the child up for adoption? I think I'm correct in the belief that most people would say, "Of course not." At that age, mom and dad have already had five years to bond with their baby. Would that parent ever look at their suffering leukemic five-year-old and say, "Had I been able to predict this, I would have had an abortion"?

But suppose a predisposition for leukemia could be detected in the womb? Leukemia could hit a family like a 9.0 earthquake—but devoted and loving parents continue to struggle amongst the rubble. There are some diseases and disorders that can be identified in utero. Having Down syndrome diagnosed before birth is like having weeks to prepare for the quake—and the preparation itself could bring the tremors down to an adventuresome—and kinda fun—3.9.

With early detection, parents can be prepared for the difficulties that might lay ahead. Children with Down syndrome will, most likely, have various delays in mobility and speech. Knowing this information before birth can allow parents the time to find resources of physical, occupational, and speech therapy.

But early detection doesn't require aborting the fetus. I feel funny saying that, considering my history of clinic defenses, protecting doctors from extremists trying to break in and close businesses which provide abortions. But in this particular case, my opinions stand unwaveringly decided. Knowing that certain special steps can be taken to promote success for the child with Down syndrome should be empowering for the parent, not a reason for eliminating one of the better population of humans from the world.

A potential mother might say, "I'd never be able to handle raising a child with Down syndrome." Really? Try raising a teenager. Every healthy child is going to eventually become a teen, and the information that adolescents are bad news is widespread. But this fact doesn't prevent parents all over the world from making baby after baby. I'd much prefer to spend extra time with my child learning how to balance a check book or follow a bus schedule than pass the hours with a teen who is giving me the silent treatment and doesn't want to be seen with me in public because I'm a dork.

My goal, although it would be detrimental to adoptive mothers like me, is to have every mother overjoyed when her child is identified as having Down syndrome. That would bring a lot more Down syndrome into the world, due to fewer abortions. It would also create a ton more happiness in the world. I wish no mothers had to mourn the Down syndrome diagnosis, but celebrate it.

As I told my friend Atusa, this is how the conversation would go if my doctor told me my unborn baby had Down syndrome.

DOCTOR: I am sorry to have to tell you this, but your baby has Down syndrome.

ME: Oh my God! [loud screaming and crying]

DOCTOR: I understand. It's very hard news to hear.

WALTER: No, you don't understand. She's *thrilled*.

ME: *YES!!* High five! Yeah!

I've heard stories of parents being concerned that typical siblings will be negatively affected by the presence of Down syndrome in the family, just like my mother-in-law was concerned. When Phillip was an infant, I met a teenage boy who had an older brother with Down syndrome. The adolescent gazed at Phillip and whispered to me, "You're going to have so much fun." And he's been right so far.

Heidi adores her baby bro, and will regularly cuddle him and sing him to sleep at night. It took a while, but I was finally able to convince her that she cannot grow up to marry Phillip. But now she says, "Someday I'm going to meet a boy who wants to marry me and wants Phillip to live with us forever." I believe she's correct. Phillip's presence in our family has made Heidi a loving, sensitive, confident person with a keen sense of right and wrong, and I predict she'll get what she wants in life because of that. He has benefitted and enhanced her life.

And she sure won't let anyone push her around—or her brother. When Heidi was in kindergarten, I went to her school-based childcare to pick her up at the end of the day. I had Phillip with me, sleeping away in his infant car seat, tongue protruding from his relaxed lips. While Heidi wrapped up the final steps of some artwork she was creating, I overheard a fifth-grade boy say to his friend, "Hey, look at that baby. He's got his tongue out like this—blahhh..." and he proceeded to make an exaggerated mocking copy of Phillip's face. The boys impersonated Phillip several times and laughed amongst themselves, looking, whispering, and pointing.

When Heidi came back to me with her completed drawing, I told her,

"See that boy over there?"

"Yeah, that's Bad Ryan." I remembered Heidi's tearful accounts of bad schooldays caused by a big boy who was the campus bully. He and his toadies generally spent their free time teasing and tormenting everyone else at school, including Heidi. Her classmates had dubbed the gang leader Bad Ryan.

I told her, "He was making fun of Phillip," and I explained what Bad Ryan had just orchestrated.

With this news, Heidi's expression slowly set into an angry sneer—I could almost hear her growl. Slowly, she turned. Even though he was over a head taller than her, several years older, and feared throughout the school, she walked over to Bad Ryan and said,

"Were you making fun of my baby brother?"

Bad Ryan ignored her.

"Because," Heidi went on, "I thought I heard you say, 'Look at that stupid baby over there.'"

Never making eye contact, he turned away, muttering, "No. No."

"I don't like it when people are mean to my brother."

"I wasn't."

Heidi came back to me and said, "He didn't do it."

He wasn't tough enough to man up to his mockery, but I was certainly proud to see my girl stand up for her brother. Because of Phillip, she defeated one of elementary school's greatest foes: bullying. Bad Ryan never bothered her again.

I've also heard about people who are worried that a child with Down syndrome would have no future—no job, no house, no significant relationship. However, in the district where I currently work, there is a school to teach vocational skills to young adults with developmental disabilities such as Down syndrome. At this school, students learn skills like furniture repair, culinary arts, landscaping, car detailing, textiles and e-commerce. With care and training, people with Down syndrome can get meaningful jobs, then go on to live in group homes, apartments with roommates, or even alone.

20/20 did a story, "Against All Odds," about a husband and wife, Sujeet Desai and Carrie Bergeron, both with Down syndrome, who live alone in an apartment. And they are not a fluke. Successful adults with Down syndrome are popping up all over the place. A young man, Lee Jones, learned to drive, got his license, earned a bachelor's degree, and travels the country lecturing to large audiences about Down syndrome. Tim Harris owns a world-famous restaurant, Tim's Place, in Albuquerque, New Mexico, and he has Down syndrome. Professionals and parents are realizing that when people with Down syndrome are not left in institutions with no stimulation, they can do great things. Phillip may never rise to the level of a Tim Harris, but we don't know what the future holds; Tim Harris may never rise to the level of a Phillip.

In the late '80s, there was a TV show called *Life Goes On* about a husband, wife, and three kids, one with Down syndrome. I loved that show and watched it religiously every week, going home early from social events to ensure timely arrival in front of the set for the newest episode. I've tried, unsuccessfully, to find DVDs of all the seasons because of one particular episode about developmentally disabled couples in love. It was so many years ago that I can't remember anything about the particular show except for two things. First, there was a man and woman sitting on a couch, a real-life developmentally disabled couple, and they were holding hands. I remember the woman having absolutely no expression on her face, her jaw slightly slack and eyes glazed over. But when her man said, "The only woman for me is this woman right here," her mouth slowly morphed into a lopsided grin as she responded, "And the only man for me is this man right here." That moment touched my heart so deeply and emotionally, that it instigated the second memory I have of that episode—my sobbing. The love of that couple was so perfectly pure. Now that I have a developmentally disabled son of my own, I can't wait for the day when he finds a love as pure as the one on that episode of *Life Goes On*.

Phillip's joy of life is so deep and heartfelt that when he grows up and knows romantic love, he is going to shower some lucky lady with devotion. And he deserves that experience. If he wants to get married someday, I will be his biggest advocate and the world's best wedding coordinator. I'm looking forward to seeing every aspect of Phillip's future, and I have no doubt that it will be bright and full of love.

In truth, I wish everyone the joy of a little bit of Down syndrome.

I'm not an angel, and adopting Phillip didn't make me a saint. By adopting a child with a disability, yes, I did want to attempt, in my own small way, to do a good deed. As one of the many who want to do something to make the world a better place, I chose adopting an unwanted child. However, I also chose one of the easiest disabilities in existence. True, Down syndrome brings with it a range of challenges, including possible heart disease, bowel dysfunction, thyroid abnormalities, and lengthy hospital stays. But Down syndrome also regularly includes an inclination for the enjoyment of music, dance, humor, and miles of hugs and kisses. Animal enthusiasts know that a lion is one of nature's most beautiful creatures, but the rare, surprise white lion cub is a glorious, unexpected miracle. Human mothers know that newborn babies are priceless; giving birth to an infant with Down syndrome is a rare surprise, a miraculous accident, worth millions to the family and the world. If I really wanted to do actual good, I would have picked a child like those in the home where I worked when I was 16—a child who would never walk, talk, see, hear, or use a bathroom, let alone know what a toilet is. My son, although I'll encourage him to strive for more, will at least grow up to graduate from high school, learn to follow a bus schedule, get a job, and pay bills. And, along with the profound satisfaction of watching him succeed, I will have the magnificent opportunity to see him foster my daughter's development into a caring, accepting, loving young woman and give my husband unconditional love that makes his life a delight to live. And I got the most adorable, red-headed, loving little dude in existence.

The baby we were planning to adopt would have Down syndrome, but the child who came into our family was a cute, funny, energetic, playful, loving baby boy, throwing a ball, taking a bath, eating ice cream, sweeping the floor, influencing and brightening our lives. He became our adorable little boy, the neighborhood cutie, best little brother, adorable grandson, heart-warming child.

I am infinitely blessed.

Chapter 26:

Fate

As the celebratory party at the park wound down and guests gradually began saying their goodbyes and heading for their homes, I couldn't help but take my dad aside and get in one good jab.

"You said it wasn't meant to be. Well, see?" indicating, with a sweeping hand gesture at the adoption party around us, "It *was* meant to be!"

His understandable response: "Did I say that?"

I grinned, my eyes wide and index poking him in the center of the chest, and teased, "Yes, you did! And I've been waiting and waiting to finally say, 'I told you so.'"

Dad meekly offered, "Well, sometimes people try to think of something to say when someone's upset…"

I cut him off and gave him a hug. "I know, Dad." I was aware all along that he was only trying to find some words to help get his only daughter through a tough time. I was positive that what he said was said with love.

But I still liked finally getting to say it out loud.

Phillip was meant to be.